Leaders are talking ab

"In *Permission to Glow*, Carter lights a new path toward working on oneself first, and then translates that into leadership at work, in society, and in our daily lives. Read it. Practice it. Live it."

MARK T. SMUCKER, president and CEO of The J.M. Smucker Co.

"Freakin' EPIC! Do not be fooled by this book. Kristoffer Carter has written a book to help leaders lead. But really, *Permission to Glow* will help all of us truly live. And though he is a man, what he's written is a deeply feminist manifesto. Surprisingly rich in insight and bubbling over with inspiration, this book is far more than it seems."

ANI DIFRANCO, artist, activist, and bestselling author of *No Walls and the Recurring Dream*

"What if everything that matters about work—making a difference, taking creative risks, earning real money, and, most of all, great success—could be handed back to you as a deeply satisfying spiritual practice? Kristoffer Carter brings the mind of meditation to his vast experience in coaching conscious leaders to offer four fantastic permissions. *Permission to Glow* shows you how to bring forth your true gifts, not by 'hacking' or 'crushing it,' but by allowing your natural brilliance to express itself."

SUSAN PIVER, founder of the Open Heart Project and bestselling author of nine books, including: *The Hard Questions, Start Here Now*, and *The Four Noble Truths of Love*

"We desperately need spiritually awakened, ethically grounded leaders who are humble enough to keep growing in wisdom, compassion, empathy, and the strength to empower others. *Permission to Glow* makes a vital contribution to the development of a new breed of leaders."

PHILIP GOLDBERG, bestselling author of nine books, including *The Life of Yogananda* and *American Veda*

"If your job is to impact others, this book is a must-read. *Permission to Glow* meets you where you are and elevates your leadership to new heights. Kristoffer Carter takes you on a spiritual journey that will enrich, challenge, and offer you the gift of powerful growth!"

NETTA JENKINS, VP of global inclusion, Unqork

"In a world full of competing priorities and pressures, *Permission to Glow* reminds us to show up for ourselves first so we have the chance to also take care of others. Kristoffer Carter makes an airtight case to hit the pause button."

BRITTANI SHAW, chief people officer, Litera Microsystems

"Kristoffer Carter is an executive coach and meditation teacher who understands leadership as a spiritual practice. In *Permission to Glow*, KC unleashes a simple framework that seamlessly supports the integration of self and Spirit—and it's contextualized for today's leadership environment."

KAREN WRIGHT, MCC, founder of Parachute Executive Coaching and author of *The Complete Executive* and *The Accidental Alpha Woman*

"This book outlines a simple, powerful path to being an impactful leader and a valued contributor. *Permission to Glow* takes coaching a huge step forward by daring all of us to show up fully—permission by permission, practice by practice."

DEBORAH JOSEPHS, chief people officer, Latch

"*Permission to Glow* does something extraordinary. It crystallizes what's at stake for organizational leaders while encouraging all of us to step forward in our work and lives. It's an insightful, powerful, and even playful integration of ancient yogic principles and modern wisdom. Ambitious. Inspiring. And better yet—it's fun."

JONATHAN FIELDS, author of *Sparked* and host of the *Good Life Project* podcast

"*Permission to Glow* is an in-depth guide to living and leading with more spaciousness, intention, and courage, so that those you lead may do the same. I have been lucky enough to work with Kristoffer Carter as a client, and our work together changed how I view both my professional and my personal life. He frames leadership in a way that draws us closer to our inner worlds, needs, longings, and, ultimately, our power and joy."

LISA CONGDON, artist, storyteller, and entrepreneur

"This wonderful book conveys a deep truth: since we're the source of our panic and overwhelm, we can also give ourselves permission to create peace and power. *Permission to Glow* guides you to channel the source within so you can lead the people around you with wisdom, compassion, and clarity. It's fun, sneakily radical, and timely for the world we're evolving in."

CHARLIE GILKEY, author of *Start Finishing* and founder of Productive Flourishing

"Finally, a leadership book with a soul. Powerful, irreverent, refreshing, and so timely. The 4 Permissions will change your life if you let them."

LAURA MCKOWEN, bestselling author of *We Are the Luckiest* and founder of The Luckiest Club

Permission to Glow

A SPIRITUAL GUIDE TO EPIC LEADERSHIP

PERMISSION TO GLØW

Kristoffer Carter

PAGE
TWO
BOOKS

Some names and identifying details have been changed to
protect the privacy of individuals.

Words and music to "In the Light" on page 160–61 by
Kristoffer Carter, © 2021 This Epic Life, ASCAP.

Cataloging in publication information is available from
Library and Archives Canada.
ISBN 978-1-77458-158-2 (paperback)
ISBN 978-1-77458-159-9 (ebook)

Page Two
pagetwo.com

Edited by Kendra Ward
Copyedited by Crissy Calhoun
Cover design by Taysia Louie
Interior design by Nayeli Jimenez
Interior illustrations by Matt Horak

thisepiclife.com

*For Amanda—and every emerging,
conscious leader like her. May we continually
awaken to find you running things.*

CONTENTS

I0822417

Welcome to a New Season

We can follow a path back to meaning and fulfillment with the 4 Permissions. Vocation elevates
our work, giving us meaning and, by extension,
fulfillment. It's easy to lose ourselves in fast-
moving demands. When we remove the struggle
for survival, we experience peace. At the heart
of our struggle is a craving for peace. But what do
we do with it?

WELCOME TO A NEW SEASON

THE 4 PERMISSIONS

HOW MANY life lessons did you first learn in Little League? Or maybe, like me, you were decidedly unathletic. Despite my limited skills, I was rapt with attention as my coaches dropped classics like:

Bring it in.
Take a knee.
Nice hustle out there; you're playing with tons of heart.

Something's missing, though. Do you feel it? What do you think it is?

There's no question we've entered a new season. The entire game seems to be changing. Our teams are different. The rules have changed. All eyes are on us, on leaders, for our plan to win.

But last year's plays don't seem to work. Or when they do, we feel more burnt-out and beat-up. The stakes feel higher and the headwinds are stronger. So, we work longer, or we disengage altogether. Our relationships fall out of balance. We carry more noise and pain around.

What game is really being played here? Where's the peace of mind? The joy?

I'm an executive coach and meditation teacher. I coach leaders at various stages of their journeys, from start-up entrepreneurs to Fortune 500 executives, from the C-level to their high-potential successors. My clients often begin by addressing capacity issues in their leadership, such as their relationship to time and what needs to be accomplished. From there, we work on accessing their full power as a business asset. They can be founders running the gauntlet of Series B financing or new leaders of billion-dollar revenue streams. I also play with the (traditionally known as) human resources side of their businesses, since my job is to help maximize the impact of their people. I work with chief people officers to design and lead meditation training for companies as big as AT&T and Avery Dennison and as scrappy as the latest financial technology start-up.

In the coaching industry, there can be more coaches than clients—and usually not enough self-care habits to support either. If I have a formal business plan, it's to build Trojan horses. But what's inside isn't some plotting, violent force. I wheel coaching and meditation up to the gates of organizations. What I'm hoping they discover inside that decoy are compassionate insight and self-discipline—what people long for yet aren't sure how to ask for. As a coach, I help expand the consciousness of leaders, and as a meditation teacher, I help organizations ground into the expanding consciousness of the planet. Trouble is, the strains of "expanding consciousness" in organizations often show up as disruption, which can be experienced as anything from mild frustration to destabilizing uncertainty. On my best days, my commitment to spiritual practice ignites that spirit of practice in those I coach. My hope is that in this book you'll discover your own path to practice. Our rapid-change pace of life can be smoothed and softened by our simple commitment to practice. As we do, our capacity expands to make room for more of everything we need and deserve.

In my earlier career in sales, I took up meditation to help compress the emotional highs and lows of the job. As meditation practice began working for me, coaching became a logical progression. Helping others exit their own struggle bus and find their path was a calling even before I was formally trained.

Coaching is about standing out on a shaky ledge together—staring down the chasm between the opposing cliffs of *what is* and *what will be*. It's the client's choice whether we build a ramp, find a vine, or jump a car like the Blues Brothers or Thelma and Louise. As my meditation practice strengthened, so did the call to coach others. Early on, it was to share what I was learning. Lately, it has been to stand in awe of

Life and business are infinitely expansive to the degree we're willing to grant ourselves 4 Permissions.

everything we discover together: that life and business are infinitely expansive to the degree we're willing to grant ourselves what I call the 4 Permissions.

The leaders I coach don't need permission to do or accomplish more. They're pretty solid on that tip. Their next horizons live inside themselves and extend outward in every direction. Their next levels are rooted in being.

Like an all-you-can-eat buffet, our world is constantly giving us too much of everything to be with. Our work, then, is to expand our container. To transcend the crazy train of disruption by using everything life offers as fuel to glow. These 4 Permissions organize and pare down our work as our world gains complexity:

Permission 1: Permission to Chill

Essentially, to be with what is—the noise and distraction of an ever-changing landscape, open space, and everything else in between. Just be. Our vast range of options, the space "between stimulus and response."[1] We can and must expand that space.

Permission 2: Permission to Feel All the Feels

To be with our full humanity—the guidance our body speaks through our emotions. The torrents and the droughts. Just feel it all.

Permission 3: Permission to Glow in the Dark

To be with our full power—the audacity of living and leading from our divine purpose, regardless of our fears.

The discovery and deployment of our full self-expression. Sufficiently and audaciously ourselves.

Permission 4: Permission to Glow in the Light

To be with our full power while standing in the full power of others—transcending competition for cooperation. Being with the work before us. Uplifting and rescuing our human family from itself.

The permissions are an organizing principle for the shifting demands of leadership. Modern life moves in dynamic pulses like a roller coaster. The forces that hold us back have always been there. They are just speeding up and gaining intensity. It's exhilarating one second and rattling the next. We can expect and adapt to these external forces.

In the pages ahead, you'll find prompts to expand your awareness. These are intended to help you pause, to reflect on how to allow in more space, light, and connection. You'll also find simple practices that align with your expanded awareness. These tools have the goal of activating the 4 Permissions. Grab your favorite journal, or scribble all over this book. Record your insights as you move, permission by permission, toward expanding your capacity. The space we create together will give all of your goals a fighting chance.

A quick word on goals. My guess is you have a Big Honkin' Dream. We all do. Can we agree that life could be sweeter if we called our goals our Big Honkin' Dreams instead? Like a satisfying workout or chiropractic adjustment, the invitation is to allow the 4 Permissions to work on you, your leadership, and your life. Give yourself permission to chill on all of your goals for a minute. Distinguish them for what they are: Big Honkin' Dreams.

Each permission activates the internal forces that create our experience. As it does, it empowers our relationship to external forces. This is like strengthening a muscle over time through repetition and resistance. External forces all but guarantee our expansion, provided we don't curl into a fetal ball for too long. Our teams, infrastructure, and markets expand to meet external demands. Our expansion as leaders, however, is an inside job.

Leadership is the space we hold for others

My friend Katie recently said, "Oh. Your book is for leaders? I don't have any direct reports." She doesn't. I'm envious. What's kind of funny is that Katie is married to a CEO. What piques my curiosity is that Katie wields infectious levels of love and enthusiasm. Two undeniable qualities of leadership that can pretty much enroll anyone in doing anything. Especially her husband, the CEO. Having a role in an organization isn't a prerequisite for leadership. It reaches far beyond any job title. Leadership happens in the space we hold for ourselves and others. Leadership is discovered in our willingness to feel into our gaps: our internal chasm between what is and what will be.

When we tend to our internal work, we step forward. Regardless of whether people are behind us just yet (or ever will be), we lead. Expansion exists in our relationship to our own power. When we strengthen that relationship, we unleash the collective power of others. Those others may be our friends, our kids, or our neighbor who wakes us up daily with a leaf blower. Purpose-driven living pulls others up and calls them forward.

Also, the 4 Permissions have been applicable and valuable to every business leader I've worked with. So, read on, leader.

The 4 Permissions guide you through the ascending gates of claiming your power. Think of them like the source fader on a DJ's mixer. Sometimes you may prefer the predictable white noise that plays in the elevator. More often, you need to fade over to those ambient jams you know will get you moving. No one but you will grant you these permissions. Refusal or failure to do so is settling for your default strategy. Settling means you're on autopilot.

Living by default, in contrast to wielding our power, is also a beautiful part of being human. It's important to love our inflatable autopilots. It's just that autopilot feels a bit more like listening to Muzak.

We are wired to default to what makes us feel safe. The predictable, the status quo, our comfort zone. Our default behaviors may still produce the desired

Leadership is discovered in our willingness to feel into our gaps: **our internal chasm between what is and what will be.**

outcome. However, we'll likely come up short on meaning and fulfillment. In the DJ analogy, our defaults are more like that crappy soundtrack that blasts at Old Navy, and the source fader of our conscious awareness takes us back to our throbbing club banger—*the music of our spheres.*

The frenemies within

Would you like to meet your defaults? As a coach, I spend a lot of time with these Wile E. Coyotes. We have a corresponding default for each of the 4 Permissions; I lovingly call them Speedy Rabbit, Game Face, Phantom Pest, and Dark Star.

Speedy Rabbit
This little beast is constantly spooked into moving faster than everyone else. Short on patience and quick on action, Speedy Rabbit can't help but judge how slowly everyone else is moving. They already went down that road, did all your thinking for you, and grabbed more Starbucks on their way back. "Permission to Chill?" says Speedy Rabbit. "Are you lazy, delusional, or both?"

Game Face
Game Face keeps it real cool. So cool, they are, in fact, impossible to read or ever fully know. They mask their humanity until they boil over into a tantrum. Their Game Face goes right back on like a gladiator's armor.

Smiling like a suburban housewife from the 1950s. "You missed it," deadpans Game Face. "I think I just felt one of my feels."

Phantom Pest

Like a cunning saboteur, Phantom Pest refuses to be fully seen, heard, or felt. They vacillate between an overgrown false modesty and swooping in to make their presence known. Their power may be felt in fits and starts but remains mostly hidden to themselves. This is a liability to the people they lead. When it's time to glow, they poof.

Dark Star

Well defined by the good people at Oxford, a Dark Star "emits little or no visible light. Its existence is inferred from other evidence, such as the eclipsing of other stars."[2] Dark Star is the antimatter of team players, a void that wanders the galaxy alone, even in a crowd. They stay hidden behind intentions like "I'm holding space for everyone," but their determination to go it alone keeps everyone at a ridiculously safe distance. Dark Star's inability to receive light is their greatest obstacle, and opportunity. The light of others seems to threaten them, which makes it nearly impossible to receive, much less glow in.

Speedy Rabbit, Game Face, Phantom Pest, and Dark Star: these slippery fish can be highly effective at producing certain results. They believe they're being helpful. When left unchecked, these defaults protect us from everything we fear, which unfortunately includes our Big Honkin' Dreams and deep connection with others.

They are usually well intended. And, just as in high school, frenemies can sabotage us only when we don't love ourselves enough to tune them out. Some version of these critters may be running things for us in this moment, overprotecting everyone from the impact or legacy we're capable of. There's a sadness in that; unless we move beyond these survival mechanisms, we'll never get a true glimpse of what we could create.

EXPAND
YOUR AWARENESS

Look for yourself in these rascals: Speedy Rabbit, Game Face, Phantom Pest, Dark Star. Which of these come out to play for you?

Simplify and amplify

The permissions are a path of transcendence for these wild times. They are a lens to view leadership through, an internal dashboard of your singular abilities and gifts. There are just four gauges on this retro instrument panel.

Transformation in our leadership, and all the results those shifts produce, isn't as simple or clean as deciding to be different. We don't metamorphose as dramatically as a caterpillar. Transformation is negotiated daily, in our willingness to grant ourselves the 4 Permissions. They whirl within and around us, daring us to make a different choice. We commit ourselves to practice. We let circumstances indicate which permission is needed, and we receive its many gifts. In our willingness to choose beyond our default patterns, we tune out our frenemies and slide that source fader over. *We begin to glow.*

Early on, our paths may be lit by mentors, a hunch, or research. As our leadership transforms, we light our own path. We silence the noise with intuition. We integrate the counsel of our feelings. We step out beyond our darkness as we learn to dance with it. Our glow attracts allies, investors, and raving fans. The moment-to-moment choice to defer to our better angels—to relax, to feel, and to glow—creates microtransformations that accumulate and compound.

"You are different," they will say. And they will be right.

Through daily practice, we'll walk the path from default to intention, from expanding our awareness to aligned action, and from intention to transformation. My goal for us is to adopt a new prism to focus our leadership through. I say "us" because I live in practice and refinement right alongside you. As I coach leaders and train organizations to implement these principles, I see

The 4 Permissions

guide you through the ascending gates of claiming your power.

both how far we've come and my glaring gaps and opportunities. Each of us has a front-row seat to our defaults—and to our highest potential.

In the beginning there were Capitalized Words

In these pages, you will run across references to God, Divine Mother, Spirit, or All That Is. I get that many of us (myself included) have baggage around these words. I have no agenda to draft you into any religious doctrine. But stripping the spiritual core out of meditation, yoga practice, or business practice, for that matter, limits our knowledge to intellectual understanding and quick-fix tactics. Our goal in meditation, and I believe in life, is to move beyond our busy minds to get to the soul. To embody something more than the storm of conflicting thoughts.

Whatever the "G-word" points to doesn't care what you call it.

My guru (yes, I have one of those), Paramahansa Yogananda, teaches that we are tiny waves on a vast ocean of consciousness. We are extensions of that consciousness, and we can feel its presence through diligent, regular practice. This has been my direct experience. We might call this consciousness God, the Universe, Jah, Yahweh, Allah, or what Hindus lovingly call Divine Mother. As in, "If your dad seems unap-proachable, go ask your mom." Divine Mother is the feminine aspect of God, the all-loving Mother of all creation.

Yoga at its core means "union"—of our individual-ized consciousness with something far greater. On our best days as leaders, we experience that union. The 4 Permissions are rooted in ancient yogic science, but the practice isn't dependent on a belief in a god to produce benefits. References to spiritual forces are my friendly reminder that we can tap into something far more powerful than our busy little minds can conceive.

As a coach, my job is to connect you with your power. I take that responsibility seriously and will do this by any and all means available. Go ahead and call "that thing" your Higher Self or your Essence. Your imaginary friend Shmanky. The Greatest of All Time (G.O.A.T.). Again, it doesn't care what you call it. My goal for us both is to feel, and then to gain direct perception of it. These are the foundations of yoga. And also of glowing in the dark.

I've got a fever, and the only prescription is . . .

We can't hope to glow in the dark in any sustainable way without Permission to Feel All the Feels and, first and most crucially, Permission to Chill. We may burst into flames at that spot where stressful circumstances, unrealistic demands, and too much caffeine converge. (Do you frequent that spot?) But before we apply the healing balm of the first permission, we need a clear picture of what all of this is for.

As leaders in a dynamic landscape, we have a big itch to scratch. What calls us forward on this path of inner and outer development? Is it just those dollar bills and prestige worldwide?

Did you see the *Saturday Night Live* skit in which Christopher Walken is producing the band Blue Öyster Cult? Jimmy Fallon and Will Ferrell are in the recording booth. "I've got a fever," Walken says. "And the only prescription is..."[3]

Look around. The world clearly needs more cowbell. And, our inner journey pursues something far greater.

If these wild times are the fever, the only prescription, or antidote—believe it or not—is peace.

THE PEACE WE CRAVE

WHAT GOT you excited about your current role? Anytime I ask an organizational leader or entrepreneur this question, I get mixed reactions. A series of blinks with crickets chirping means no strategy or forethought has been given to their current role. They just ended up here, like that time Forrest Gump met a few presidents. Too often I get the opposite: performative "excitement" overlaid with some corporate talking points. This is a slightly different version of "I just work here" from the first example. They're not being deliberately disingenuous. There's just a disconnect between what I experience as their success and however they experience it. Almost like they are selling themselves on being excited.

Other leaders answer that question with a genuine crackle of excitement, from some place deep within. There's a reverence, a wonder. A sense of deep gratitude and understanding of their mission, either to their customers, their team, or both.

All the peace a vocation gives

How we answer that question also depends on who's asking the question, and how full our plates are. One answer I've never received is, "I'm excited about *all the peace* my role creates in my life."

And yet, when a leader is fully present in their contribution, so much more than the job title is in play. A sense of mission elevates their role to a vocation. In rare cases, vocation is a mystical (potentially mythical) realization: *I'm doing the thing I was born to do.* In more common cases, it's knowing they are in the "right seat, on the right bus" (with due props to Jim Collins and *Good to Great*[1]).

Finding ourselves in the general vicinity of our vocation is sweet relief. That internal voice quiets down and stops asking if this is the job we should be doing. We don't ask ourselves if the gig is good enough for us, or if we are good enough for it. We allow ourselves to be more connected to the work itself versus evaluating our experience of it.

I don't know about you, but when I'm too in my head, my internal dialogue sounds like a never-ending

DVD bonus commentary mixed with the sloppier aspects of Comedy Central's *Drunk History*. Boisterous, disjointed, and incessant.

However, when I'm leading from vocation, I am at peace. This includes feeling at peace in times of daunting workloads, when challenges are everywhere, and balancing all of it with life beyond work.

Silencing the inner dialogue has launched many epic spiritual quests. At first, we try all sorts of quick fixes aimed at quieting it down or shutting it up altogether:

> *The drinks.*
> *The mindless scrolling.*
> *The eating of our feelings.*
> *The staying in constant motion, or "shark energy,"*
> *as I refer to it in coaching.*

We have a hunch that it's possible to work super-hard for something we love—while having our heart satisfied at the same time.

This direct experience of vocation—without head trash, justification, or apologizing for it—is *the peace we crave*. Hard days and hard years happen. Still, this could be the work we chose and the work that chose us. Peace is in there, even in the most challenging years. A life spent constantly moving too fast (Speedy Rabbit), unable to tap our authentic excitement (Game Face), blind to our power (Phantom Pest), and unable to fully receive the contributions of everyone around us (Dark Star) is too high a price. There will be no peace. Just the push for what's next.

Silencing the inner dialogue has **many epic spiritual quests.**

EXPAND
YOUR AWARENESS

How do you know when your soul is present at work?

Can spiritual practice and business coexist for you?

Who has the prior year prepared you to show up as in the next five?

Where peace shows up

We won't find peace until we consider a radical notion: *it is peace that we crave.* I'm not implying peace at the cost of success or of the leadership and management our teams require. I'm talking about peace in addition to every other external measure of success. I mean *at peace* inside, as we continue to move dynamically and glow brilliantly on the outside.

> *At peace with what shows up in the moment to test us: Permission to Chill.*
> *At peace with what wells up in our hearts to guide us: Permission to Feel All the Feels.*

At peace with what the world is asking of us:
Permission to Glow in the Dark.
And at peace with the whole of our human family:
Permission to Glow in the Light.

However the past decade has treated you, it made one thing clear: we live in an age of unlimited possibilities. Something with a far better sense of humor than we have designed this existential obstacle course we call "life on Earth." And as intense as it can look and feel, there's a beautiful allure in seeing how it all turns out.

Life is a deafeningly loud thriller at some points of the day and can be the perfect rom-com by night. We complain about it, we dance with it, and at times we even conquer it. It beats us up, and we still can't shut it off. We bear witness to all of its broken beauty and, in our finest hours, to our own transcendence.

Somehow, despite all the damn racket, we manage to accomplish much of what we set out to do. We're lucky if we realize we're doing exactly the thing we came here to do. But those "awake in the dream" moments are fleeting. They blow in and out like summer storms.

We get to be both our favorite heroine and favorite villain. Our player levels up when we are aware of how the game is shaping us. The game tests us by asking us how badly we want the Big Honkin' Dream.

Media headlines rarely inspire us as often as they outrage or paralyze us. Never before in human history has there existed such a violent contrast of high-stakes reasons to change, packaged with an overwhelming number of options for how to do so. Sprinkle in some random chaos and misinformation, and the game gets harder to navigate.

Our eyes dart frantically across seemingly infinite choices, from careers to lovers to breakfast cereals. Our ears hear the wild success stories of friends who swore it was impossible just five years ago. Exotic aromas of global supply chains waft down small-town Main Street. We taste the potential of an ever-increasingly small, interconnected world. We just can't seem to leave our screens long enough to touch it.

It's a wild world of possibility, just on the other side of countless potholes, obstacles, and distractions. The show is so viscerally real that it ratchets up our senses. We notice those we care about moving at a perpetually frazzled clip.

Venti everything with a side of Flamin' Hot Cheetos

We may have been raised on a diet of "they who are the fastest win," but our need for speed comes at a high price. We miss things we once held dear. We fast-forward our partners, our friends, and our kids through their stories when we ask how their days went.

There is little to no satisfaction in simultaneously chasing yet somehow missing everything. The tempo has become so all-consuming that we fear the downshift and dream of coasting. By this point, *The Greatest Show on Earth* starts to look like *Mad Max: Fury Road*. A lot of wheels are flying off, explosions and potential threats are everywhere, and there are no signs of a break anytime soon.

Our senses have been trained into a relentless, unsustainable tempo. This has become our new normal and we've made sacrifices. Remember when contentment was a worthwhile pursuit? It fit nicely somewhere between equanimity and sufficiency, where enough would quite pleasantly be *enough*. But for the Fury Chasers, contentment feels more like complacency. We can't stomach the absence of doing or competing or achieving. The pace itself has broken our emotional palate, like eating a bag of Flamin' Hot Cheetos before sitting for your Master Sommelier panel.

There's nothing wrong with being the fastest or getting the most stuff done. Our experience of time speeds up as we move through our lives. We sense our potential to make a unique imprint during our time here. The problem lies in the frenetic, high-octane static we drag with us into every room.

Western culture does an outstanding job of maximizing everything. There was a time when most people didn't consume gigantic buckets of coffee or soda all day long and into the evening. When we could wait in lines without screens entertaining us. Parents take their kids out to trick or treat with booze in travel mugs. Everyone loves a good party, so now start-ups have bars built into their office kitchenettes.

At what point do we hit pause and ask ourselves: What's going on here? **What are we so desperately distracting ourselves from?**

At what point do we hit pause and ask ourselves: *What's going on here? What are we so desperately distracting ourselves from?*

Are these the spoils of modern life or tools of mass distraction? We deserve to be comfortable. We work hard and sacrifice for our toys. And yet these addictive creature comforts wedge themselves between what we want to experience and what we're able to feel. They reinforce some janky story that we need twenty levels of awesome to earn one fleeting moment of peace.

We're becoming more attuned to the difference between what actually nourishes us and empty calories. The rat race is so 1980s. Many of us have figured out how to show up in the office when we want to, how to design a better career, or how to create more impact with no office whatsoever. Compensation for our time comes in many forms, and although the mighty dollar keeps our lights on, it is meaning and fulfillment that keep the fires burning.

This is not another book about getting what you want. Permission to Glow is about getting what you need—meaning and fulfillment. Don't worry, Speedy Rabbit. Meaning and fulfillment are the foundation of you getting what you want more consistently.

Our human experience is a situation comedy with plenty of drama and suspense. At some points in our journey, when exhaustion peaks, we sense there's another way. We feel the path pointing us upward, toward vocation. It feels more spacious. It's a path that's uniquely ours, which liberates us from the comparison and shame that come with the constant push to achieve more.

EXPAND
YOUR AWARENESS

What is the most dramatic or chaotic area of your life?

What is that a distraction from?

On a continuum with "Dead Battery" on one end and "Full Power" on the other, where is Peace for you?

We crave it for good reason

Peace pauses the chase. It creates space and includes long exhales. Peace frees us from striving and restores contentment as a worthy ideal. Call me an old-timey hipster with a handlebar mustache and a monocle, but I've always dug the simplicity of Earl Nightingale's definition of success: "the progressive realization of a worthy ideal."[2]

When we're at peace with ourselves, we're able to accept the beauty of our singular path. Already in progressive realization. We stop placing our self-worth on the other side of achievement, or our sense of accomplishment on someone else's checklist. We seize little moments of awareness and notice how blessed we are. All the battles we fight with ourselves are settled in one radical act of surrender. We hear the boisterous yelling everywhere. Still, we choose peace.

As in our outside world, inner peace may never be permanent. We trip over it when we run out of things to worry about. We're at peace when we remember we're living the lives that we chose (and bonus points if we would choose those same things again), and during those magic moments when all the people in our lives aren't obstacles but allies.

In moments of peace, we may realize:

Here are my laundry lists of challenges and shortcomings, and here also are my access points to unlimited power and creativity.
These are the souls I get to travel with. Those are the souls I get to serve.
Here are the qualities I am here to express, which, by the way, were a gift intended to be shared. I don't need to "earn" my right to express, share, or glow.
Here are my divine gifts I get to pay forward in service of humanity.

We watched in horror as our world exploded into protest, sparked by the incomprehensible death of George Floyd at the hands of law enforcement. Signs

held up everywhere read, "No Justice, No Peace."
People are doing their best to march in peaceful protest,
through a gauntlet of racial tension and lines of soldiers
dressed in tactical riot gear. Is peace even possible in a
world of extreme volatility?

The end of the fight against systemic racism may be
a long way off. The injustice in America alone has been
centuries in the making. Still, generations of leaders
who created lasting, positive change did so through
peaceful means. They were willing to endure horrific
brutality and injustice in their peaceful resistance,
because it was less painful than living in the broken
status quo. Martin Luther King Jr. ate dinner with his
beautiful family beneath a photo of Mahatma Gandhi,
a portion of whose ashes are interred in Yogananda's
World Peace Memorial on the coast of Los Angeles.

Peace is in no way a soft leadership skill or some
wimpy ideal. It takes unbelievable strength to disengage
with the dark inertia of armed conflict. In the same way
brave change agents are making a stand to end injustice, we must also give ourselves the radical reprieve of
peace. The alternative is being a Fury Chaser. In discov-
ering peace within and around us, the unsustainable
pace becomes sustainable, and we settle in for the long
haul.

Peace gives us compassion, and vice versa. Self-
compassion allows us to repeatedly forgive ourselves for
not being perfect, for being too much, or for denying
ourselves love and respect for any slight infraction.
Our lack of self-compassion shows up as constant

The 4 Permissions are the personal consent we've been waiting a lifetime for, only to **realize it has always been ours alone to give and receive.**

second-guessing, comparison, or riding ourselves like some crappy little horse jockey.

If you believe in any benevolent force that holds the universe together, you might consider the whole motivation within Fury Chasing is that we may notice, and eventually crave, peace. When we are at peace, our schedules, resources, and adjacent possibilities expand. We're no longer limited to the crisis in front of us.

Choose a path, and walk it

Peace can be considered our ability to accept what is. It doesn't mean everything is quiet and beautiful. When we're nonresistant, we can see our circumstances, warts and all. We release attachment to the way things *should be*, so we can notice them the way they are. In this sober awareness, we can then get back to creating *what will be*. We can choose to be calm in a chaotic moment or find ways to laugh at the messes we create. Then, from that peaceful detachment, we can reclaim our curiosity and creativity. In not resisting what is, we conserve valuable power, which can be redeployed constructively. Releasing attachment is a crucial, ongoing practice.

As we perceive peace beyond some passive state of acceptance, we experience the fiery force for good that it is. We discover new paths of getting there. Moment to moment, peaceful potentials appear as choice at the individual level. We can choose to quiet the storms. Decide to drop the panic. Maintaining peace and navigating back to it becomes the work.

There are proven paths to peace that have endured thousands of years. The Buddha walked his path around 2,500 years ago. Jesus Christ built the spiritual foundation for Western civilization 500 years later. More than 2,000 years prior to Buddha, the ancient rishis of India, accomplished and enlightened sages at the peak of a golden age of civilization, discovered the science of yoga. All paths are profound and will get you to the destination. All deserve deep study and practice of their essential truths. We will not compare or evaluate spiritual paths here. Your best path is the one you will remember and use regularly to get to the destination. That Supreme Peace doesn't care what you call the path back to it, let alone which path you take. Your sincere effort will always be rewarded.

A path to power, through peace

The 4 Permissions are a path that starts in the interior of the individual and ripples out to the farthest reaches of impact across our human family. Each of the four is unlocked through regular, diligent practice. Each permission produces success in and of itself. Like yoga, there are no limits to how far you can walk each of these paths. They will keep opening like a thousand-petaled lotus, willing to give whatever you've expanded your container to hold.[3]

The reason the 4 Permissions work is actually quite simple. They are what our souls require of us. Nothing more, nothing less. Practicing each permission expands our capacity to be with and hold more. To exceed your potential and all expectations, pick one and get started. Relax into your skin and take breaks from the clock. In other words, chill. Listen to and empower the subtle guidance of your feelings. Feel all there is to feel. Express what you came to express, despite your fears. Glow in the dark. In your consistency, you will attract compatible allies to achieve a higher purpose, or glow in the light.

Each of the 4 Permissions shares aspects of what our soul expects—expansion. In their simplicity and through our dedication, we will be led down our path. Deny yourself the permissions and suffer complexity, distraction, and exhaustion. As in meditation, by practicing releasing the static, we'll eventually find the signal. By staying attuned with the signal for longer stretches, we may find some day that we are one with it. Union, or yoga.

Permission requires authorization, or consent. But we're done asking anyone else. Only we can grant ourselves these permissions. We're blessed when anyone takes a moment to awaken our possibilities. However, when it comes to the 4 Permissions, they are lessons we need to teach ourselves. They are switches we must find the audacity to throw. They are the personal consent we've been waiting a lifetime for, only to realize it has always been ours alone to give and receive.

They are called "permissions" to remind us to exercise our human will and tap into our divine will. Most of us grow up asking for a time that's convenient for everyone else, or for approval that whatever we're doing is enough.

I'm nudging you to consider what could be. To make the push toward creating what will be. Nudging you so that, from now on, you show up having already given yourself permission at any and all four levels. No more approval by committee. No need to prove worthiness. Once you've taken the first few necessary steps of activation, you can then nudge, inspire, and uplift others to do the same.

Invocations are used to summon presence. They are activations. There are no hardened hearts or skeptical minds that can't be opened by reason, practice, and repetition. When I was a child, a TV evangelist conned me into fearing all things spiritual. As a seeker, I found better teachers. If we're willing to open ourselves, as humble practitioners, we may find grace in any passing moment. Eventually we may perceive grace as The Container, holding all we conceive of. From whirling atoms to galaxies. Our stressors and limits vanish in that vast benevolence.

We grant ourselves the 4 Permissions.
Each is unlocked through practice.
Unlocking any one is transformative on its own.
However, there is cumulative, compounding power in
practicing all four.
This isn't theory. It is testimony.

Permission 1 on deck: Permission to Chill.

Modern life moves at the speed of VUCA, the military term for volatility, uncertainty, complexity, and ambiguity. Claiming our power begins with slowing down this crazy train. The Permission to Chill is symbolized by the pause button. Conscious reprieve. Effective leadership requires light-touch, high-leverage actions—despite any noisy headwinds. Discernment becomes crucial. Meditation strengthens discernment.

PERMISSION TO CHILL

PAUSE BUTTON
SYMBOLOGY

OUR TEENAGE daughter recently discovered an ancient artifact. I blew the dust from its case and cracked it open. "We called these *cassette tapes*. They contained music, sometimes collections of hand-selected songs."

"You mean, like, a playlist?"

"Better, my child. Mix tapes."

Mix tapes were their own art form and are probably best explained by John Cusack's character in the film *High Fidelity*, adapted from the excellent book by Nick Hornby: "Now, the making of a good compilation tape is a very subtle art. Many do's and don'ts. First of all you're using somebody else's poetry to express how you feel. This is a delicate thing."[1]

Part of that subtlety is the production. This wasn't dragging various tracks into a playlist like some pampered savage! You were recording tracks from vinyl, CDs, or other tapes onto a fresh cassette. To do this seamlessly, you relied on the pause button. It helped create a clean gap between tracks. The record function would stay engaged, and then you un-paused playback for the length of the track.

Another ancient relic also had a pause button. This had much larger cassettes and was called a VCR, or video cassette recorder. The first VCR remotes were connected by a long cable that wasn't quite long enough to reach your sectional sofa. The remote became a deadly tripwire, one the cat couldn't stop messing with. Up to that point, broadcasting as we knew it ran everything on a program schedule. Meaning, if your butt wasn't in front of the TV, you were going to miss your show. The pause button provided the power of choice. We could choose when we were ready to view or listen. We could choose when we wanted to record it and watch it later. The pause button gave us the power to say, "Hold up there, Powers That Be. I'll consume your content when I'm good and ready."

Never to be confused with stop, pause is a momentary break in the action. Stop says, "We are done here," while pause says, "I need a minute." Stop would end the movie experience and pause would freeze the frame, allowing you to pick up where you left off.

Through the endless slipstream of information, pause is our sword and our shield. We can silence the chatter, halt, and redirect to what better serves us. We pause to look up what was said, to fact-check its authenticity. We can pause communication and relationships and pick them right back up, whereas stopping cuts them off entirely.

Pause is our gateway into the gap, and our exit point back to the action. When the children entered the wardrobe in C. S. Lewis's classic book, Narnia awaited while their world stood still. Pause gives us reprieve from the current onslaught, or the power to hold on, or savor it a bit longer.

Like meditation practice, the pause is a deceptively active process. But when you become consciously aware that there is a pause button in any circumstance, and that only *your* finger can activate or deactivate it, you realize the gravitas of the quote: "Between stimulus and response there is a space. In that space is our power to choose our response. In our response lies our growth and our freedom."[2]

Pause. Chill. Drop back into the mix with more wisdom and discernment.

INVOCATION

I can and must hit the pause button.

In the frenzied pace of life, to chill is a holy, defiant act.

Creativity and breaks from suffering all come from creating s-p-a-c-e.

I create space in my schedule, between each thought, and between each breath.

I chill to remember who I am and what I'm capable of.

I do my best to meditate daily.

TO CHILL
IS DIVINE

SPEEDY RABBIT might be the fastest, but that doesn't mean she loves the game. There is constant self-judgment in thinking you should always be moving faster. Also, judging the pace of others doesn't earn much love or respect.

When we're triggered into busyness, we confuse our self-worth with our output: the more we produce, the more valuable we are. We start judging everyone and anything that gets between us and getting more done. No one is ever doing enough. Overwhelm hangs steadily in the background. Anxiety takes the wheel.

Relationships suffer. Trust is eroded down to cynicism and blame. Exasperated, under-slept, and pitting out in our finest pantsuit, we think, *But I'm winning!*

Are we?

It takes a lot of energy and action to build a business. No one disputes this. But not all energy or action is created equal. More energy, hours, or action doesn't always produce better work.

Energy and action have a point of diminishing returns. Once we blow past it, the quality of both drops. We seem to be running on fumes or a hollowed-out caffeinated sugar buzz. Action becomes less focused, and we're likely to jump in and do someone else's work.

There's a paradox I see with the more seasoned leaders I coach. The demands on their time and attention continue to expand, and somehow, they keep optimizing toward more light-touch, high-leverage activities. This requires a commitment to living outside the weeds. A commitment to moving ahead despite the current ordeal, or to not waiting to take a vacation until the giant project ships. They create the chill space before, during, and after high-demand periods and projects. They don't push rejuvenation into the future, once they're in the clear. Space is allowed for increased demand.

Keeping it chill doesn't always mean golfing in the middle of a workday. There's no shame in that game if that's the case. A relaxed tone and pace get tenderized into these leaders over time. Does that wisdom have to come with age?

They accept that things can get frantic. More often than not, they choose calm.

They have given themselves Permission to Chill.

The greater the volatility, the more determined we must be to **slow down and make better decisions.**

If our default is action, to chill is divine

Permission to Chill is a mindset and a practice. It's an understanding that as our world speeds up, we can't be as effective if we're going Speedy Rabbit right along with it. The greater the volatility, the more determined we must be to slow down and make better decisions. But this counterintuitive mind frame isn't something we can just decide to have one day.

The mindset is forged in consistent practice. As you practice slowing down and hitting the pause button (especially in chaotic circumstances), you will find the simpler, more direct path forward.

Our commitment to being chill provides access to the mental and emotional bandwidth needed to handle problems. It also develops the intuition to proactively solve them. Paramahansa Yogananda called this "right action." Action for action's sake is tiresome and wastes time and energy. The (chill) leader of right action is willing to slow down. She chooses the appropriate response to the problem at hand. In doing so, she is much more efficient, and more time is gained. A seasoned leader reinvests that time into creating more s-p-a-c-e.

Think of your life as a painting. From the outset, as you envisioned your completed work, you began with a white canvas. The master artist knows the value of the blank space needed to create the piece. Permission to Chill creates appreciation for the negative space. It becomes the canvas we paint our lives on. Moment to moment, we're setting a foundation for what follows.

Committing to spaciousness won't solve all your problems. At first, you'll be more present for just how messy some of your problems truly are.

Doing the most does not equal fulfillment. There's a paradox in how we spend our time. When we overidentify with the doing of things, our soul is left unfulfilled. Stuff will always need to be done. Often, we may be the only one to push it forward. But when we pack our days with task lists, and overschedule ourselves hard-start to hard-stop with no time for transition, we get locked into a cycle of suffering.

Even if we're fortunate enough to love our work, when we're overscheduled, we develop tunnel vision that compromises relationships, disconnects us from our purpose, and leaves only tiny pockets to squeeze the rest of our lives in. The anxiety that follows chants a mantra of "I have no time" as the noise of the outside world gets louder and louder.

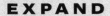

EXPAND
YOUR AWARENESS

What are you committed to creating today?

Notice that I didn't ask how much time you had to create it.

IF CHILL IS THE BALM, VUCA IS THE RASH

OUR WORLD is speeding up and gaining complexity. The military has an acronym for the ever-changing nature of warfare:

Volatility
Uncertainty
Complexity
Ambiguity

There's mild relief in knowing someone created an acronym for whatever *all of this* is. Volatility, uncertainty, complexity, and ambiguity are like an aggressive rash. Chill is the balm. Think about today's headlines. Our outer world carries a tempo and temperature that seduces our stress response. The twenty-four-hour news cycle is amplified by social media. Everyone we've ever known may weigh in on how VUCA affects them. The background static is distracting at best and crushing at worst.

Even if we aren't looking for it, VUCA comes and finds us. Prior generations had their share. Still, our current level of intensity feels like the pinnacle. If it's not catastrophic weather, it's a global pandemic or constant political division. Our high-VUCA world has billions of other shoes; any one of them can and will drop at any second. All of this static spooks Speedy Rabbit to move even faster.

Even *considering* hitting pause is a defiant act.

The outer world will continue to move with unrelenting force. We cannot stop it, but we can, and must, cycle down our experience of it. Permission to Chill is slipping out of a chaotic party for a few moments alone on a quiet balcony. The downshift from overstimulation to a self-imposed bubble of peace can be jarring. The louder our environment, the louder our internal dialogue becomes to protect ourselves. When we defiantly choose silence, we can perceive the gift of space. When we notice ourselves as something separate from the noise, we free ourselves from the stories about what the noise means.

Gaps appear, and in those gaps is the actual experience of life, free of interpretation. This experience of oneness is what we're after. We are blessed to trip over it in fleeting moments. Holding our newborn child, lying beneath a bowl of shooting stars, or periods of flow beyond clock time. Those beautifully connected moments are usually felt as a truer reality, free from the splintering overwhelm of the senses.

It feels real, but look closer

What we call *reality* is a canvas already covered in brushstrokes. Each stroke represents an interpretation of what's going on. Some are made by us, and many are made by others. The media we consume, societal norms, trusted experts, and so on. We form more interpretations as we process what's coming at us. All day long, we paint over interpretations with more interpretations, and as a result, we get a little further from a pure perception of reality—that oneness, when we are fully embodied.

We're given a blank canvas each morning when we wake up, and once again we reach for the paintbrush. Without a pause to consider the wider canvas, we forfeit our creative power and layer on more interpretations—one degree further removed from objective truth. Without a break from adding to the noise, we stay glued to the noisy screen. Our world is then whatever the media tells us it is. Distant relationships become limited to posts in our newsfeed. Everything is reduced to the algorithmic story we've already been feeding ourselves. Nothing quite glows.

Speed through life without enough chill time, and you'll become well acquainted with overwhelm.

Speed through life without enough chill time, and you'll become well acquainted with overwhelm. Our cycles of boiling over come back around whenever our cache gets too full of to-dos, interpretations, or indecision. We end up with less time than problems to solve.

Overwhelm and a perpetually darkening sense of what's real wasn't the original goal. We learned to keep our heads down and our noses to the grindstone. (Can we please retire this horrific expression?) We bought the lie that taking breaks was another way to lose. We equated our self-worth with how busy we were, how swiftly we could perform, despite any obstacles in our way.

We limit our sense of self to what we've overcome. Survival. We play the victim or the hero. In either role, we're separate from our experience of life, judging everything like a critic walking through an art gallery. Access to our power (our glow) remains hidden. Trapped in a binary funhouse of mirrors.

What to trust: the head or the heart?

Despite its estimated eighty-five to one hundred billion neurons, we can't always assume our brains are the best filters. Our hearts start beating roughly twenty-one days after conception and beat unconsciously (without our awareness) for the duration of our lives. The heart is our engine room, beating 100,000 times every day to circulate more than 2,000 gallons of blood.[1] Sleeping or waking, it beats around three billion times over an average lifespan, circulating blood through 60,000 miles of veins and arteries.[2]

Our brain misinterprets perceived threats at work, often escalates unwanted outcomes, and keeps squawking to justify all of it.

> *My board thinks I'm a hack.*
> *Any delay in closing this deal means it likely won't happen.*
> *Her feedback is a veiled personal attack.*
> *If I don't deliver by the end of today, my career is over.*

What makes us assume these thoughts paint a clear interpretation of reality, let alone serve us?

The brain's processing power is unparalleled. It is constantly reevaluating, reinterpreting, and rerouting based on new information. However, when our super-computers are left on and the cache is never cleared, performance suffers. We assume our brain's assessment of what's happening is all there is. Our heads drown out our hearts. There's too much noise to sort through. When our minds become our only reality, we live from the ego. A healthy ego helps get big things done. Left unchecked, an unhealthy ego runs amok. We get fixated on the binary swings of victim or hero, with me or against me, and act as Judge Judy of right or wrong. An unhealthy ego wants us to lose.

Our head and heart are both vital to navigation. We tend to defer to the head when receiving guidance from both simultaneously. Wisdom is the integration of both. Clear thinking from the head, gut-checked by what our heart knows as truth. Our brains think thousands of thoughts each day, and more often than not, this faucet is left on unconsciously. Our hearts and minds are doing their jobs all day long. One is literally keeping us alive, and the other only thinks that it is.

Conscious, constructive thought leads us forward. Heart-centered actions do the same. It's the filtering and sorting of too much information that causes over-whelm. For most of us, staying lost in the wilderness of too many thoughts is easier than stepping out on a quiet balcony for a breath.

The high-VUCA landscape trains us to stay in the fight, and our bodies to stay tense. Without breaks from the constant processing, the tension hardens and becomes part of us. Beliefs become rigid truth, and our hearts get hardened. The irony, biologically at least, is that we're evolving to become more malleable. More adaptive, and more agile. We need to step back from reacting to all this VUCA. Instead, we might reflect on what our high-VUCA world is asking of us. Staying in the battle with no breaks feels like shoveling quicksand. It's exhausting.

EXPAND
YOUR AWARENESS

How does VUCA show up in your life and in your business?

What is it asking of you?

DISCERNMENT IS WHAT WE'RE AFTER

O NE MAY assume that hitting pause is a passive process. It's not. Permission to Chill must come first because the stakes couldn't be higher. In the gaps between all the busyness and overload, we take our breaths to keep swimming. We may also find a path to becoming the highest version of ourselves. Without time to pause each day, can we be sure we're not regurgitating someone else's interpretation, spouting their wisdom, or living someone else's script?

We won't conquer our high-VUCA world by running ourselves ragged. Nobody's winning by fighting against it. If we allow it to whip us into a frenzy, we're only adding to it.

Finding calm in a noisy world can be simple. Soothing ourselves is not some strange, unattainable concept. We've been biologically wired to self-soothe since infancy. We just forgot how as life sped up. The moment you realize no one is coming to save you from your jam-packed schedule is the moment you can sit down and take a couple of deep, defiant breaths. The slightest gap of space creates a preference for more.

If there are millions of stressors in modern life, there are also millions of ways to chill. Practice expands the space around you, which allows your life to create itself. The most direct path to being chill is creating a simple, daily meditation habit. Meditation increases neuroplasticity, our brain's way of adapting to our evolving needs in life.[1] Meditation can also be more restorative than sleep.[2] As a practitioner for the last fifteen years and a teacher for the past eight, I believe the biggest benefit isn't what is usually cited.

Meditation strengthens the key quality we need to navigate and ultimately transcend our high-VUCA world. Discernment.

Discernment is a vaccine for the VUCA virus.

Meditation clears the static between our little self (our bodies and minds) and our higher self (our soul). Discernment tells us where we are operating from. Whenever our busy world grabs our attention, it's our meta-attention that sees what's really going on, and what our adjacent possibilities could be.

Meditation strengthens the muscle of our meta-attention, allowing us to get back to being, and off the hamster wheel of doing. Discernment helps us notice the mind's unconscious river of thought-vomit. We can now shift our perspective from doing too much to the sufficiency of being enough. Or from feeling down in the maze to being up above it. From living our lives in half-baked interpretations to pursuing truth.

Discernment is a key component for the peace we crave. It's at the heart of the "Serenity Prayer."

Serenity isn't limited to recovery

A couple of blocks from my office in Akron, Ohio, is the founding site of Alcoholics Anonymous. AA has used the "Serenity Prayer" as a healing mantra, guiding hundreds of thousands (if not millions) of people through recovery. But prior to the prayer's adoption by AA, reverend and theologian Dr. Reinhold Niebuhr wrote it to calm soldiers during the Second World War.

Dr. Niebuhr's prayer was adapted and simplified into the "Serenity Prayer" we know today. Read it from the perspective of navigating our high-VUCA world:

God grant me the serenity
To accept the things I cannot change,
The courage to change the things I can,
And the wisdom to know the difference.

Discernment is "the wisdom to know the difference." Our internal compass will point us forward once we take stock of what, if anything, can be changed. Discernment guides us from victim consciousness into personal agency for what we're here to create. I've seen a simple meditation habit upgrade all other self-care habits and conquer lifelong anxiety and addictions. All through discernment. As in, "Does this serve me?"

Alcoholics Anonymous is regularly criticized for directing its members in recovery to a Higher Power, especially in steps two and three of its twelve steps.[3] If we get over its spiritual overtones for a moment, we can see the path to serenity is our own commitment to walk it each and every day, to cultivate that wisdom (discernment) through daily practice.

The peace we crave, our transcendence of VUCA, lives in our commitment to practice. AA's reinterpretation of Dr. Niebuhr's prayer has saved countless lives. Its application extends far beyond addiction recovery. Discernment extends to self-actualization and uplifting our planet. Serenity is that oneness, that completion. Free from the hammering of VUCA.

Our ego misidentifies our body, accomplishments, or failures as *who we are*. Through consistent meditation over time, we find we're more than our first person, physical perspective. We catch glimpses of our higher aspects, and we may even access the massive, full iceberg of our soul. To find that higher vantage point, we need to nurture that relationship the same way we would any other. It takes commitment and consistent communication.

Our ego misidentifies our body, accomplishments, or failures as **who we are.**

Squandering our days digging in someone else's sandbox is missing the opportunity of a lifetime. Our glow stays hidden beneath mountains of static when we listen only to the direction of others or are guided unconsciously by fear.

Think about your closest relationships. Picture the faces of your beloved family and friends. Would you ever want to be thought of as volatile? How do your actions create either uncertainty, complexity, or ambiguity for those you love? As we surrender into the gaps, we find our own rhythm. We relax into the waves, which makes it easier to catch one and, God willing, ride it.

Prolonged uncertainty takes its toll. We project our worst fears onto others, and decide whether they are with us or against us. We settle for the binary. Our assessment of others is futile and exhausting. Speedy Rabbit resorts to judgment, criticism, and many failed attempts at control. Eventually, Speedy Rabbits find everyone they've ever known rotating through the hot seat.

Ready or not, it's time we chill

In the United States, we overcomplicate creating a meditation habit the same way we overcomplicate everything else. Too many choices and conflicting information. You don't need another app. In fact, you will become a much stronger, consistent meditator if you focus on the essentials.

It took me five years to create a consistent daily habit, and another five to commit an hour every morning. You can solidify a habit in well under thirty days. We're going to make this just like brushing your teeth, except I'm not going to yell at you if you miss a day; nor will I ask to smell your breath.

Sitting consistently for just five minutes per day—every day, no excuses—will potentially upgrade all our other habits. Thirty-five minutes of silence per week may not sound like much. It isn't. But it is enough to strengthen our willpower and discipline. This sets the stage for increasing to ten, then fifteen minutes per day, every day. Our goal for our meditation practice is to build to a minimum of fifteen minutes every day, no excuses. One hour and forty-five minutes per week is now more time than most people spend in church, or in connecting with their intuition. It also primes us to give ourselves the other three permissions.

Many people find that after thirty consecutive days of meditation, they feel a subtle difference when they miss a day. Something feels a bit off, and they feel more complete once they sit down to meditate. By this point, there's a root system forming beneath the surface. This structure has some of the benefits mentioned above. We preserve our integrity. We improve at hearing what our bodies are telling us (Permission 2: Permission to Feel All the Feels). This strengthens our discernment so we can pull back on undesirable habits, and people, and find more supportive ones.

In meditation, by bringing our attention back as many times as necessary, we flex and strengthen our meta-attention. Although it's nice when it happens, the goal of meditation isn't the absence of thought. Our goal is to become aware of those thoughts, to release them, and to bring our attention back to an anchor point. Our anchor point could be our breath, our heart-beat, or a mantra. Thoughts will continue to float across the screen of our awareness. Noticing how often this occurs can be exhausting. However, if we're determined to practice, there's no limit to how many times we can clear the screen. Remember: every successful clearing of thought, and reclaiming your attention, is one rep in building your meta-attention muscle.

Meditation: Break it on down

Whether you're sitting for five minutes or five hours, a meditation session can easily be broken down into three necessary phases.

PHASE 1: GETTING YOUR ATTENTION

Right as you sit, roughly 5 to 10 percent of your session time can be used to claim your attention. This is done through breathing exercises. Start with simple 4-7-8 breathing cycles. This simply means to inhale deeply through the nose for a count of 4, hold for a count of 7, and exhale fully and slowly through the mouth for a count of 8.

This technique works because you're forcing a specific breathing pattern onto the involuntary nervous system. This is that squirrely part of us that VUCA gets in a twist. Four cycles of 4-7-8 breathing takes about fifty-seven seconds. (If you don't have fifty-seven seconds, you have bigger problems and you may be beyond hope!)

Sit up straight and expel all the breath from your lungs. Whether seated in a chair or cross-legged on a floor cushion, relax the body. Picture your posture adjusting into straight lines (chin and shoulders parallel to the floor, as well as your thighs if seated in a chair). Your spine should be as straight, or perpendicular to the floor, as is comfortable. Place a hand on your abdomen to help feel how deeply you're breathing.

Inhale deeply for the count of 4

Breathe through the nose, expanding the chest and lungs, and take it all the way to the base of the abdomen. Feel your hand move out on your deep inhale. Make this the most nourishing breath you've taken all week.

Hold for a count of 7

It doesn't have to feel strained, or too long. Simply count a bit faster, but be sure to keep the counts even. You're reminding yourself that you are in control of your breath. The ghost in the machine. Once you remember this, your thoughts should calm down considerably.

In meditation,
by bringing our
attention back as
many times
as necessary,
**we flex and
strengthen our
meta-attention.**

Exhale fully and slowly for a count of 8
*Breathe out through the mouth. Making a deep "ah" or
"om" sound as you exhale will also help you relax.*

This breathing pattern is powerful because you are
deeply oxygenating the body, while getting your own
attention.

PHASE 2: HOLDING AND RECLAIMING YOUR ATTENTION

The bulk of your meditation session (up to 80 percent of
the session time) will be in this phase. This is where the
real work of strengthening your meta-attention happens.
If you skip the first phase of getting your attention, this
phase will be much more difficult.

There are many techniques we can use to bring our
attention back. Beginners usually start by watching the
breath or scanning different parts of the body.

Mantras are helpful because they give the busy mind
a task. The repetition is calming, like needlepoint or
running. Many of my students have found success with
our sky mantra:

I am the sky—watching all weather move through me.

An even simpler one would be:

This is what it feels like to be free.

Your mind and ego will throw your attention around
like a mechanical bull. This is the sometimes tedious
but necessary work of meditation. Notice the thought.

Drop it. Redirect back to the breath or to your mantra. Reclaim your attention. Your power. As many times as necessary.

PHASE 3: DIRECTING YOUR ATTENTION

Once you've claimed your attention, then spent valuable time holding and reclaiming it, you deserve some reward for your effort. Directing the attention is something we get tempted to do during the second phase, when we should be dropping thoughts and reclaiming focus. Often our creative muse shows up, with no shortage of great ideas.

Other than a mantra, it's helpful to hold back any pointed, directed focus until the end of the meditation session. Another 10 percent of the total meditation can be devoted to savoring and directing our efforts.

I recommend starting with gratitude. In yogic meditative practices, this is usually the point where the meditator has done the heavy lifting of clearing their head, and now lifts their focus from material concerns into a higher state of consciousness. Bask in the glow of your effort. Set intentions, pray, or chant. Direct your freshly cleared attention to offering deep gratitude for every aspect of your life. Savor and maximize the feelings of oneness you've just created.

Clearing the static

When we're un-meditated, we're more likely to let circumstances affect our moods or trigger snap judgments. We interpret a setback as proof that we're failing. We take a partner's gentle reproach as hostility, and we shut down for fear of creating a similar response. We assume our teammate's tardiness is passive-aggressive or blatantly disrespectful.

When we're actively clearing the static session by session, day by day, we develop a wider set of options. We access ways of being that are more in line with the soul. Though our mind and ego may be begging us to blow our stack, we regain composure. From there, we pivot up into gratitude, focusing on the things around us that bring us joy.

Our awareness has returned. We are now better able to be with what is. We may notice more support and creative options than when we were drowning in VUCA. Maybe we now have a slightly more spacious canvas.

Maybe now we'll be better able to hear what our feelings are telling us.

Awareness + Practice =
PERMISSION TO CHILL

1   **In a journal, answer each of the Expand Your Awareness prompts in this section.**

2   Do one-minute reboots throughout the day. Complete four cycles of 4-7-8 breathing. Inhale deeply through your nose for 4 counts, hold for 7, exhale slowly through your mouth for 8. Four cycles will take about one minute. Start with once per day and gradually work up to four reboots (of four cycles) per day.

3   Reflect:

If you weren't so busy, what would you have to face?

What is your first or next step to deepen your meditation practice?

What is your favorite excuse to avoid sitting to meditate for five to fifteen minutes?

When was your last retreat and when is the next one?

What is there right now for you to release or surrender?

Our feelings are a strength. Feelings are projections of root emotions, which help steer us toward what we want. When we allow ourselves to feel, we embrace our humanity. Permission to Feel All the Feels connects us to ourselves, to others, and to All That Is—symbolized by the unicorn, which reminds us our magic doesn't need to be visible to be present.

PERMISSION TO FEEL ALL THE FEELS

UNICORN SYMBOLOGY

I N AMERICA at least, unicorns jumped the shark when Starbucks issued their atrocious drink made from pink and purple foamy chemicals. Most recently, unicorns have infiltrated every facet of our lives, usually as annoyingly cute, rainbow-and-glitter-farting cartoons.

This pop-culture flash point was decades in the making. In the 1980s, there was the dramatic cartoon feature *The Last Unicorn* (its title character representing purity in a dark, dangerous world). Kids who grew up in that era may have tripped over the magical photography of Robert Vavra's coffee-table book from 1983, *Unicorns I Have Known.*

My mother was obsessed with this book, and for good reason. There are photos of various unicorns in all climates of the world, presented in perfect photo-realism. The book lived on my mom's coffee tables for decades, and poring over it, I could feel the author's love of the mythology, symbolism, and history of these creatures. The photos are truly stunning, and even today look absolutely authentic.

Central to the unicorn's mystique—and our cultural fascination—is their singularity. They are completely uncommon, the cute explanation being they must've missed Noah's Ark. In our world of knowns, there's something alluring about an impossibly exotic beast.

The unicorn symbolizes the balance of grace and swagger, of magic and mystery. Its possibilities rekindle our little-kid sparks, make us smile, and invite our innocence back to the table. We are once again steering a pirate ship or braiding daisies into a long, lustrous mane.

Allowing ourselves to feel all the feels is access back to innocence. Speaking the language of our hearts reclaims our humanity, and listening to it restores our guidance system. Our ego grows strong and loud into adulthood. The ego hijacks our emotions and pounds them into armor.

Feeling creates that rare, mystical exception to the rigid rules of adulthood. With our intuition as truth, and our scattershot feelings as whispers from our Divine Mother, we find contentment on our journey. The cynical and hard-judging world can play its part. We choose to be the rarest, most authentic version of us—the exotic being outside of time. A pristine diamond in all that rough.

The unicorn symbol reminds us that we have softer edges than we usually reveal. Its mane blown back, showing the speed of life. The velocity of our emotional flow. Our legendary horns shoot up from our center, what yogis and Hindus call the Kutastha Chaitanya. This is the seat of concentration, and our portal to divinity. It is where, once our minds are clear (Permission to Chill), we will summon our dreams into existence. First as our vision, followed by manifestation. God whispers to us through this point between the eyebrows.

The horn rises at a perfect 45-degree angle, pointing toward our unlimited, geometric expansion: onward, upward, and outward. The galloping rhythm of hooves builds to a gliding cantor. In a full-out sprint, nothing can touch us. That horn cuts all headwinds, like a ship's mast on a choppy sea. As we sense our internal, eternal compass, we now know which sides are port, starboard, bow, and stern. Guided by the wind and stars, we are limitless. Free.

We will go anywhere, because we already sense all opportunities and risks. We see it long before we arrive, navigating closer with precision. Feel by feel.

INVOCATION

I use my feelings to hear the wisdom my body is speaking.

My feelings point to root emotions and will not be ignored.

This guidance system is a gift from God and lights the path to my divinity.

I embrace my perfectly imperfect humanity without condition.

I choose to feel what there is to feel.

I give myself permission to feel.

GAME FACE, AND OTHER WAYS WE HIDE

OUR FEELINGS betray us all the time. A testy stakeholder sends a cryptic text, our star team member resigns to pursue her dreams, our partner asks us how we're feeling about their solo trip without us, and we say, "I'm fine." Meanwhile our vibe reeks of some emotion that directly contradicts "fine."

Maybe we're grappling with something that happened at home, and our team notices our disengagement. Have you ever ghosted someone without leaving the room?

"What's going on with you? Where did you go?"

The ability to even know, let alone name, what's competing for our attention is impressive. We usually respond to "Where did you go?" with "Oh. I don't know. I'm back now." The inability to cop to where we went is a wall. These could be our most convenient walls to hide behind all day long, like suburban homes hidden from the busy freeway. There's an exciting world of adventure out there, or a quiet and cozy space in here, but you'd never know it from the other side of the wall.

We forfeit countless opportunities for connection and vulnerability. We keep our Game Face on. Sure, it's not appropriate to let all emotions rip at any given moment of the day. Still, we overcorrect and default to Game Face even when it's completely safe to share more of ourselves.

EXPAND
YOUR AWARENESS

In a work meeting, what does withdrawing or disengaging protect you from? Consider "I don't know" a cop-out. What is it protecting you from?

Break out your full Lite-Brite, little Care Bear

With Permission to Chill, we discovered that creating space in our lives is a prerequisite for the magic to come. A more spacious mind helps us hear what our emotions are saying. When we aren't able to listen to how we're feeling, we don't have access to our full range of possibilities to glow. It's like breaking out the Lite-Brite, except without the colorful pegs. You could be so much more than a sad little black box and a paper sailboat template.

How can we play full-out if we are still hiding from ourselves? Permission 1 allows us to be with ourselves and the circumstances we're in. Permission 2, Feel All the Feels, allows us to be with the aspects of our humanity we subconsciously hide. Denying our feelings is the most common way we sabotage ourselves. It's always easier to blame the whole thing on others and stay safely hidden behind our Game Face.

Feeling is brave work. Small breakthroughs in feeling can produce big results. In yoga and meditation, working with our emotions is a process of purification over time. Even just noticing emotion is more work than most people are willing to do. Disregarding our feelings outright is a way we hide. Accepting our feelings and then navigating by them will connect us with others and move us toward what we want. Willingness to feel gives us access to our divine guidance. Owning our vulnerability is a powerful way to glow.

When we aren't able to listen to how we're feeling, we don't have access to our full range of possibilities to glow.

Our ever-evolving world is asking us to feel

Business leaders around the world have prioritized emotional intelligence as a critical area of skills development. The World Economic Forum, in its exhaustive survey *The Future of Jobs*, surveyed chief human resources and strategy officers for the skills needed to prepare for a future of massive disruption, artificial intelligence, and automation. In 2020, a list of the ten skills that all industries identify as being most crucial to the future of business included emotional intelligence for the first time, coming in sixth.[1] Just five years earlier, in 2015, emotional intelligence wasn't represented in the World Economic Forum's study.[2]

I've noticed a sea change toward pausing and looking a couple of levels deeper in the organizations I work with. When we're not getting the full story of what someone wants, we can feel the tension between their words and their energy. This isn't sorcery. It can be sensed with reflective listening—sharing what you're hearing in your coworker's silence. It can sound like the subtle tightness in your friend's voice every time they mention an upcoming performance review. It could be the tirade of complexity a CEO brings to a particular subject that frustrates them.

Genos International is a leader in the emotional intelligence assessments and training space. It summarizes EQ, and its critical importance, as follows:

Emotional Intelligence (EI) or emotional quotient (EQ) is a set of skills that help us better perceive, understand, and manage emotions in ourselves and in others. Collectively they help us make intelligent responses to (and make use of) our emotions. These skills are as important as your intellect (IQ) in determining success in work and in life. Everyone, no matter what job function, has interactions with other people. Your ability to notice your feelings, understand them, and how they impact the way you behave and relate to others, will improve your "people" skills and help you ultimately be more satisfied and successful.[3]

Dr. Brené Brown's research on shame and vulnerability has created a tidal wave of interest as well as hard data that proves emotional intelligence can't be written off as a soft skill. EQ is critical to being an effective human being, and it's good for business. As our culture grapples with systemic racist structures, toxic masculinity, and patriarchy, creating safe and open conversations is more important than ever before. Screaming at coworkers is no longer acceptable. Emotional pressure isn't an effective motivator by a long shot.

Leaders who work on fine-tuning their abilities to express and read emotions are creating far more positive impact and enjoying greater success in organizations. Modern business is a dynamic landscape, swirling with existential threats and unlimited potential. To sail those choppy seas, you're going to need your entire crew. But we can't hope to reach others without reaching fully into ourselves and then sharing what we find.

Check-ins, a practice evangelized by Conscious Leadership Group (CLG), are becoming commonplace. Meetings begin with each leader around the table taking a moment to share the thoughts, feelings, and body sensations they are bringing into the space. This happens prior to discussing the intended outcome of the meeting. The expectation of a check-in is to be as authentic and vulnerable as is appropriate to the setting. This helps level the field by reminding everyone that we're bringing more than our Game Face or corporate posturing. As each person shares, the room opens to greater relatability and trust. Collaboration and decision-making can then move forward from a place of mutual understanding, rather than from disengagement or surface-level status updates.

We make feeling wrong something to be avoided

In life, few things trouble us more than how we feel. Some of us lock up our feelings and bury them, never to be seen again. Others treat percolating emotions as inconvenient. *What is wrong with me?* we ask as we shed a few tears. We apologize for our slightest emotional response, as if it's some heavy burden to witness. Whenever our feelings grow too large to predict or control, we assume something must be wrong.

This isn't like me. Where is this coming from? Our feelings can break in larger waves. They have a lot to say, and they want to weigh in on all topics. Too often we default to judging ourselves for how we feel, instead of taking the time to decode what we're feeling or what that's telling us. We make "ugly crying" something to be made fun of. In our clever self-deprecation, we forfeit the opportunity for self-inquiry.

Unfelt feelings grow into a noisy wash of static that hums constantly in the background. Throughout our workday, the energy we need to do our jobs comes and goes. Certain tasks energize, while others deplete us. It's rarely the task itself that is depleting but rather the feelings we have about it. Just like the dripping faucet of unconscious thoughts in meditation, our feelings can focus us—or create a dense fog layer between us and what we want.

Feelings can also gang up on us. We have a thought of comparison while scrolling social media. Someone celebrating a fat new job on LinkedIn. Or maybe they're taking their family to Bora Bora. We may feel a brisk wind of scarcity. They must be happier than us. This triggers feelings of sadness or shame. We went in looking for a quick escape and ended up in the alternate 1985 in *Back to the Future Part II*.[4] Biff is now the awful mayor, and life sucks. It's not what we saw that made us suffer. It's our feelings about it.

My hope is that
by turning on the
faucets (even
the old, crusty,
gunk-filled ones),
**our bodies,
minds, and souls
will travel lighter.**

A word about feelings and trauma

There's a good chance Permission to Feel All the Feels may uncover repressed trauma. Please always share any and all troubling feelings with a trained professional. Consider that when uncovering trauma, permission also includes working through what you find with your licensed counselor or therapist. The feels heal. My hope is that by turning on the faucets (even the old, crusty, gunk-filled ones), our bodies, minds, and souls will travel lighter.

If you have experienced trauma, you are not alone. Life certainly deals us much more than we can process on our own. It's tragic, and incomprehensible. No one asks for or deserves it.

Our unprocessed fear, helplessness, or horror may get pushed down into our physical body, manifesting later as disease. Often, trauma scars our emotional bodies and creates cycles of suffering. Outbursts of anger or rage and violent emotional swings are just a couple of the side effects of a traumatic event. Outsized threat response to everyday stress is also common.

According to the National Council for Behavioral Health in the United States, 70 percent of adults have experienced at least one traumatic event in their lives. Roughly 223 million people. The research also estimates that more than 90 percent of clients using public behavioral health services have experienced trauma. More sobering and disgusting, in the United States, physical and sexual abuse of women occurs every fifteen seconds and every six minutes respectively.[5]

Tragically, trauma is all too common. More fuel to demystify and destigmatize the processes of working with it.

Isolation begins and can end in our feelings

We are wired to resist how we feel as protection, which is reinforced by cultural programming. The well-meaning advice Elsa receives from her parents in Disney's *Frozen* is the perfect summation of our base tribal instinct: "Conceal. Don't feel."[6] The tragedy is that this broken cultural norm holds us apart from the thing we crave the most: feeling connected, seen, and heard. If we aren't able to share how we're feeling, how will we connect with others? The less our feelings are acknowledged, the more invisible we become. We escalate into anger just to be heard, which only reminds us how unlovable we perceive ourselves to be. A cycle of suffering.

How we feel about what happened is what separates a good day from a bad day. A quiet day with few demands could be an oasis of peace in an otherwise busy week. That same day could feel like we're underemployed or not productive enough. We're bored and not working near our full potential. Binary thinking takes over. The day was great if we felt relaxed, and garbage if we felt anxious or bored. We tend to have a great day if we get along with everyone, but a terrible day if we feel bad about a single disagreement.

Our soul-level fulfillment lives in perpetual expansion and requires continual connection with others. Even a hermit monk, secluded far off in a cave, is connected with the lineage of masters who trained him, the supporters in the community who bring food and supplies, and of course, with God. If his days were spent in the constant storm of feelings and thoughts, he would've given up long ago. Through self-compassion he moves through and beyond moods, which are habitual feelings.

When we're unwilling to receive the guidance of our feelings, we wet-blanket ourselves into being wrong for how we feel. We feel bad. To feel ambiguously, generically "bad" is a cop-out and has the energy of a bratty little kid with their arms crossed. "It's going to be a bad day" becomes a decision upon waking. You're perfectly entitled to have as many crappy days as you can handle, but your soul won't settle for it. Rather than rubber-stamping everything as bad, look a bit deeper.

EXPAND
YOUR AWARENESS

Presence yourself to the day you're having. What is one thing you can celebrate?

What (if any) good is there to feel about that one thing?

A PATH
BACK TO
OBJECTIVITY

S WE fine-tune our awareness, we see life objectively. Our vastly diverse emotions are gradients on a continuum. This level of sophistication is fitting for a limitless soul traveling in a sleek bodily temple. Emotions are rooted in being and must be consulted. By contrast, feelings are mental interpretations of root emotions.

When we accept and love whatever we're feeling, we are aligned with the soul.
When we judge how we're feeling, we cut ourselves off.

When it's all too much and we refuse to feel, we are denying our humanity.

This includes all forms of spiritual bypassing. We reason that to manifest the life we want, we shouldn't succumb to the negativity around us. We should only feel happy and do our best to live a "high vibe" existence. This bias to live vibrationally high can make a lot of sense. The spiritual aspirant, fed up with feeling despondent, discovers a path up and out of their emotional turmoil.

If that road feels unfulfilling, and this new path gives me hope, then why settle for the old road?
It must be bad to feel that way. If that is bad, then this must be good.

We are caught in the binary and out comes the wet blanket. Now, at best, we're left accessing only half of our feelings. When we cut off our ways to feel, even seemingly unhelpful feelings, we put on our Game Face. We think it's protecting us. Meanwhile, the mask blocks people from knowing the real us, or from feeling an authentic connection with us. When we're unwilling to express, there's always something more going on behind the mask. A perma-grin mask is just another strategy.

Feelings are of the mind, emotions are of the soul

The terms *feelings* and *emotions* are often used inter-changeably. There are very specific distinctions between the two. Imagine emotions as roots and feelings as the tree. Emotions arise in the body and can be experienced either consciously or subconsciously. When we experience an emotional response, we may be fully aware of its origin. More often than not, we don't know where it's coming from or why we're responding the way we are.

Emotional preferences are often created and stored in early childhood. Pixar's excellent film *Inside Out* depicted the core emotions as joy, sadness, anger, fear, and disgust.[1] Research varies greatly in identifying the core emotions. Although the number of categories generally falls between six and eight, a 2017 study in the *Proceedings of National Academy of Sciences* found as many as twenty-seven, though they were "bridged by continuous gradients."[2] Your box of emotional crayons may have a handful of primary colors or a robust symphony of sixty-four.

The important distinction from emotions is that feelings are processed through the mind. The "tree" of our feelings is more visible to our conscious awareness and therefore can be pruned. An emotional response is triggered in the body, such as trembling from fear or an adrenaline spike from anger. From there, our minds take over and interpret our emotional responses into feelings.

Your box of emotional crayons may have a handful of primary colors or a robust symphony of sixty-four.

Over time, our habitual feeling responses form moods. An emotional response may be triggered only momentarily, but a mood can last hours or even weeks. For this reason, feelings provide an excellent opportunity to work our way backward to the root cause. As we get better at identifying our feelings, we can dig deeper into what they mean and how to empower them.

For example, a young leader may notice a tensing up every time a particular customer leaves a voicemail. The emotional response in his body is, "I'm in trouble. We did something wrong." Over time, they notice a growing resentment for everyone who touches (or neglects) that account. Anxiety starts marching the halls like the Stay Puft Marshmallow Man in *Ghostbusters*. Eventually the leader gets tired of dealing with the customer and the account is lost. Was it the team's performance or the leader's inaction that became a self-fulfilling prophecy?

Flipping a switch from feeling "in trouble" to being confident isn't possible in the moment. However, we can take responsibility for our emotional response and notice the paths we took toward feeling this way. When we get conscious of the patterns that justify (or contradict) our feeling, we can de-escalate the response. By working with our feeling response, people or situations that once triggered us eventually no longer affect us. We heal our response to a given stimuli, and in doing so, it no longer has a hold on us. As our healing moves into our emotional roots, we make space for more nourishing feelings like compassion and gratitude.

It's not possible to feel hatred and gratitude at the same time. This is one of the many reasons why Buddhists practice loving-kindness meditation. When we consistently play well with others, even a perceived adversary, it becomes impossible to despise them. From that place of neutrality, we can get glimpses of our adversary as a human being on their own journey. Somewhere, someone loves this challenging critter! In wishing them well, we can ease how we feel about ourselves. We may even reach a point when we genuinely love and respect that challenging critter for assisting our own healing work.

EXPAND
YOUR AWARENESS

Start by visualizing your favorite person, then someone you're indifferent about.

Then visualize a challenging person.

In their own ways, how do each of these people assist you in your healing work?

The boredom opportunity (yawn)

Boredom is the most obvious indicator for change. Leaders and overachiever types usually struggle when they experience boredom. It's one of the easiest feelings to identify and then act on. It is often a sign of an issue with your calendar. Bored leaders are either over- or under-scheduled. They haven't committed to enough activities that make them glow, so they hide behind managing stretches of stress or lethargy.

Boredom sits at the exact midpoint of the emotional spectrum. It's completely neutral, like the beige walls of a cubicle. Just above boredom is contentment or being satisfied with what is. Just beneath boredom is frustration or being dissatisfied. Getting out of boredom isn't as complex as finding some way to be joyful. Joy isn't readily accessible from the midpoint of the scale. However, getting out of boredom can be as simple as asking yourself what's in the way of contentment. This is the restless parent who hasn't taken enough breaks from their family, who decides to take a breath, and then scraps the dinner plan for something more creative. This is the under-challenged manager who reallocates their time in order to mentor others. This is the senior executive who tees off guilt-free with zero business outcome. Once we feel just a bit more satisfied, we can find a way back to feeling hope, maybe a little optimism, and up into enthusiasm.

Be wary any time you want to escape boredom. There are always more newsfeeds to scroll and videos or beverages to consume. Remember, anytime you feel a hint of boredom, you get to choose. It can be your trap-door down to the depths or your escape hatch up to the heights.

Stay in the discomfort for a moment. By taking a minute to find out what the boredom is saying, you give yourself Permission to Feel All the Feels. In feeling wherever you are in the moment, adjacent possibilities appear. You can then navigate north or south. We tend to slide down the emotional scale unconsciously but need to move up the scale consciously. Whining about boredom reinforces it. Noticing and navigating empowers us.

FEELING TO CREATE

ADJUSTING TO our feelings as they arise is a way to reclaim our power. Once we're grounded into how we feel (instead of being resistant to it), we can get back into action around our Big Honkin' Dreams. We crave healthy relationships in all areas of our lives. When we're annoyed by someone at work, it doesn't make us a bad person. It can feel more appropriate to say whatever they did made us "confused" or "mildly peeved," when it actually pissed us off. When we acknowledge our anger, we're able to better identify our unmet needs. In that clarity, we can have an adult conversation and ask about getting those needs met. At the very least, they deserve feedback on how their behavior was received.

Since our feelings are influenced by any number of internal and external factors, the practice of noticing, acknowledging, and inquiring for the unmet need helps us navigate. The alternatives are fetal-ball denial (Game Face) or letting our feels drag us around by our hair. We can also proactively design outcomes by feeling.

Whenever we're mapping any new endeavor, we can tune into what successful completion will *feel* like. Closing our eyes at the outset and visualizing ourselves holding the completed product in our hand or celebrating a massive, newly closed sale creates a familiarity with the unprecedented. It taps our reserves of current or past accomplishments and tethers the future state to something we've already conquered.

Have you thought about stepping into the red circle and giving a TED Talk? Maybe you already have, and you want your next outing to be bigger. Some of us may feel overwhelmed by the process; others, completely giddy with anticipation. Regardless of the work it takes to prepare, there's likely a bigger commitment to tap into.

Call up the feelings and emotions from your favorite moment at the front of the room. That moment you became one with your written or spoken word. When all eyes, ears, and hearts were in full support of everything you were teaching. Maybe now you can write your talk like a love letter to your most ardent supporter, while adapting the language specific to the event. Envision yourself stepping into that red circle along with everyone who has ever learned from or supported

We launch
feelings like flares
**to light our
path ahead.**

you. Your circles of connection and influence have grown exponentially. Feel that deep sense of connection and power. Tap it regularly as you prepare, and then deliver.

Designing future feelings

Permission to feel begins by acknowledging what's coming up for you in this moment. There is no judgment of good or bad, only noticing. Feelings are important indicators of root emotions, which have traveled with us and may stay around a while longer. Yet, we also know we can heal or evolve these feelings whenever we're ready. We can be just as willing to feel what best serves us as we are willing to feel the discomfort of whatever holds us back.

Our bravery in sharing our feelings—beginning and ending with ourselves—removes the outdated emotional black box approach. We grow more translucent, or what my friend Yaniv Shanti describes in his ecstatic dance workshops as "caramelized." I experience this with leaders who are fully embodied. They possess a beautiful balance of quiet power and energized openness to meet anyone where they are. "Caramelized" is that sexy combination of grace and swagger. Practicing permission to feel in trickier situations, ones in which we used to shut down, gives others the space and compassion to do the same.

Our inner landscape becomes better nourished, and the passing clouds of emotion eventually allow more sunlight. In our willingness to feel, we methodically clean our skylights. We accept that feelings are here to inform us, not to make us wrong. We can also empower our creativity by practicing future feeling states.

As we'll discover in Permission to Glow in the Dark, our bodies can't always tell the difference between fear and genuine excitement. When we breathe into the feeling states that support what we're creating, we can embody those future states prior to stepping out onstage, unboxing our world-changing product, or kicking up our feet in our new office with an incredible view. We can borrow those visceral feelings from past or current accomplishments as we place our mental and emotional bodies in an immersive simulator. Visualization multiplied by feeling. Full body priming. We may surprise ourselves when it quickly becomes our lived experience, and we think, *I've felt this before, and it's still better than I imagined.*

We launch feelings like flares to light our path ahead.

Awareness + Practice =
PERMISSION TO FEEL
ALL THE FEELS

1   **In your journal, answer each of the Expand Your Awareness prompts in this section.**

2   Explore and practice Nonviolent Communication. Regularly identifying your feelings, and the needs you have beneath them, will sharpen your emotional guidance system and de-escalate most drama in your life. Marshall Rosenberg's definitive book, *Nonviolent Communication*, is an excellent starting point.[1]

3   Create a daily gratitude practice. This releases attachment and promotes healing through sufficiency. Start by making a list of three to five things you're grateful for at the end of each day.

4   Practice self-love and self-compassion. Loving ourselves is crucial work, and we may find it the hardest practice of them all. I created a mantra I've found transformative in my own self-love work. Start by visualizing your favorite person. Then visualize people you are indifferent to and eventually people you find really challenging. Do this while repeating, either mentally or out loud, "I completely love and accept you, exactly where you are—as I completely love and accept myself, anywhere I am."

5   Listen for your whole-body "yes!" This is a conscious leadership principle that helps you interpret what your body is saying. What feels like an expansive "yes!" in your body, rather than something you should say no to? Be willing to listen to the answer.

6   Determine your enneagram number. This is a nine-number system with mystical origins. It's a multidimensional personality assessment . . . and, like, so much more! Determining your enneagram number can be a joyous quest in self-discovery. My favorite resource for all things enneagram is my friend and teacher Susan Piver.[2]

Self-actualization is the work of the soul, not the ego. By choosing the audacity to glow, we step up to deliver what the world needs from us. Permission 3 is symbolized by the lightning bolt—our full expression of power. Sharply contrasted by our darkness, and all the brighter because of it, Permission to Glow in the Dark may be translated to "permission to fully express, despite the ever-present fear."

PERMISSION 3

PERMISSION TO GLOW IN THE DARK

LIGHTNING BOLT SYMBOLOGY

LIGHTNING BOLTS recall for me some of the most dramatic memories of childhood. They were the rock stars of the summer storms that rolled in out of nowhere, with roiling purple and midnight-blue skies in the middle of a late afternoon. Lightning arrived at the fever pitch. In a preview for the coming show, God would fade and then cut the stage lights. And oftentimes the lights in our homes.

Witnessing a bolt with your eyes could be as elusive as seeing a shooting star. Or, depending on which direction you looked, you might see many jags ripping the darkness with crackling white light. Their lines as fine as lasers, but much more rock and roll, tearing up a black construction-paper sky.

Their sonic booms occasionally accompanied downed power lines or blasted trees. Strobe-lighting the darkness, the no-man's-land of corn fields and hills beyond our postage stamp yards suddenly seemed cool. Contrast was everything.

In our own lives, our full display of power contrasts the humdrum pace of life. Your lightshow may come out of nowhere, in the culmination of years of work, or by the growing intensity of raising the stakes. Our power may erupt, or steadily emerge over time.

Perhaps the most famous lightning bolt of childhood struck long before I was born, on November 5, 1955. Dr. Emmett Brown and Marty McFly knew it would hit the clock tower, because of the 1.21 gigawatts of power needed to send Marty "back to the future." It was 1985 when we learned that, apparently, lightning can fuel time machines. The DeLorean could get up to 88 miles per hour, but it was the flux capacitor that tore a hole in the fabric of time.[1]

We may need to summon the lightning in a specific moment. Other times, some higher aspect of our selves calls in reinforcements. In these transcendent moments, our full-blazing expression surprises even us. Dumbfounded onlookers may ask how we did it, and we may shrug our shoulders as if to say, "I just work here."

Having any opportunity to share our light is a gift in itself. But to consciously summon God's light to crack us open and express through us shows everyone else what's possible. Self-expression is our gift to the world, and indirectly to ourselves.

INVOCATION

My full self-expression doesn't need to be earned.

It's my joyous responsibility—in service of everyone around me.

My singular, crazy light has come for a specialized purpose.

I unleash my purpose when I blaze this light.

My darkness is only fear, which is the perfect test, contrast, and venue for my light.

Fear is a weather system that won't ever fully pass.

So, I laugh maniacally into my darkness and throw the switch anyway.

I give myself permission to glow in the dark.

DARKNESS— FEAR OR FUEL?

PERMISSION TO Glow in the Dark is our willingness to be fully expressed—despite or because of our fear, which always hangs nearby. Glowing feels defiant because it's an expression of divinity itself, not of the ego. Our ego wants to worry that we're hogging everyone else's light. Our ego remembers every time we stepped out of line as a child and the swift consequences. As an extension of Spirit in physical form, in any moment we glow, we've accepted responsibility for our mission. We are fully aware of the stakes. We just choose to stay out of our own way.

We're at peace when we're on the road to our Big Honkin' Dreams. Earl Nightingale might call this the progressive realization of a worthy ideal.[1] We're truly blessed in moments when we feel that oneness, with both our vocation and the divine timing of our becoming. Serving others in ways that creates the life we've dreamed of is like a convertible road trip (with zero traffic) up California's spectacular Highway 1. Living that dream, already in progress. In love with the work. At work with The Love. Of course, our mischievous ego covers the road to nirvana with landmines and hungry gremlins.

Light and darkness dance together. Every January in America, we reflect on Martin Luther King Jr.'s words: "Darkness cannot drive out darkness; only light can do that. Hate cannot drive out hate; only love can do that."[2] In addition to charting a path beyond heartbreaking injustice, Dr. King captured the inverse relationship of light and darkness.

Consider your light as full self-expression. Our ever-present darkness (fear) crowds around us, questioning our safety at every step. Glow a bit brighter, and the darkness deepens to jet black. To create the unprecedented, especially in unprecedented times, we must befriend the darkness. When we're confronted, judgmental, or stopped by fear, the darkness compounds itself. It drowns out our light.

When we don't give ourselves Permission to Glow in the Dark, by default, our Phantom Pest shows up. Phantom Pest sabotages us when we don't accept responsibility for shining our light. We find it much easier to project our shortcomings onto others by pestering them. This could be a leader who avoids uncomfortable but necessary conversations with her team. The withholding builds and then triggers what one of my CEO clients calls "swooping and pooping"—micromanaging the smallest details rather than driving the big picture. The power move would have been to close new investors, but instead the Phantom stays up all night choosing fonts for the PowerPoint deck.

Phantom Pest, distracted by the uncertainty of confronting their own power, hangs back in the darkness. The unconscious saboteur. Temporarily blind to their path, they chase satisfaction in lower-value work. Meanwhile, they're driving everyone else nuts.

We can befriend our inner phantom and still act. Whenever we empower a bias for "staying in it," darkness is transmuted into fuel. Are you ever awestruck by mad-genius entrepreneurs or Olympic ski jumpers? Those high-flying beasts who lean forward off their skis, sailing toward glory with seemingly zero concern? Both are still governed by gravity. Spend enough time with either and they'll reassure you:

> *The fear has been and always will be there.*
> *Growth is about getting on with the job at hand.*
> *Courage isn't the absence of fear. It's the muscle built by*
> *doing the thing anyway.*

Friedrich "Fritz" Perls, Laura Perls, Ralph Hefferline, and Paul Goodman partnered to create Gestalt therapy in the 1940s and 1950s. One goal of Gestalt therapy is to create personal responsibility through intense

To create the unprecedented, especially in unprecedented times, **we must befriend the darkness.**

awareness of what's happening in the present moment.[3] By tuning into our subtle bodily sensations, perceptions, and emotions, we can train ourselves to hear the wisdom our body is speaking. Permission to Feel All the Feels. Too often, our bodies tell us we're under threat and we should be very afraid.

EXPAND
YOUR AWARENESS

What comes up when you ask: "What is my Big Honkin' Dream?"

Does something need to be "handled" before you get to pursue your dream?

Tune in deeply to your body for one minute.

What is your most direct path to achieving your dream?

Surrender the length of a karaoke track

In his book *The Big Leap*, Gay Hendricks describes "the upper limiting belief," what we might think of as resistance to glowing in the dark.[4] He points to a curious aspect of human nature. Whenever we achieve success, or brush up against our potential, our ego smacks us down as if it were the '89 Detroit Pistons playing sand volleyball against Danny DeVito. We are just as, if not more, likely to self-sabotage when things are going very well. I liken upper limiting beliefs to that odd thing certain cats do. The ones who thoroughly enjoy being pet and scratched behind their ears, right up until they short-circuit and mangle your hand.

Upper limits show up at work constantly. These are the self-imposed complexities we add to a gigantic sale we don't feel worthy of closing. This is the coach who fills her dream client roster, only to have the scheduling system melt down. This is the (*ahem*) first-time author whose self-care wheels come off each time they pass a new milestone. Nothing provokes our frenemies within quite like living the Big Honkin' Dream. As Susan Piver recently said to me, "No one mentions that living your dream is also completely terrifying." It's a Molotov cocktail in a champagne flute of "I can see my house from here!" with the lingering gas pains of "I wonder if my crater of failure will catch on fire when I screw this up."

Our fear is our relationship to uncertainty. There is uncertainty everywhere, because we're always doing things we've never done before. Expressing our gifts takes place out in the unknown. We're not quite sure how it will turn out. We just showed up out here on our leading edge. The landscape is always fluid with rapidly changing circumstances. But if we knew how it was going to turn out, our journey wouldn't crackle and hum with new possibilities.

Permission to glow lives just beyond the safety of our comfort zone—and safely beneath our ejection seat of upper limiting beliefs. We're willing to express our gifts when we're not too spooked by the unknown or by our own power. This narrow passage is adhered to both consciously and unconsciously. To access our power, we must throw the switch anyway.

Glowing can be the culmination of a lifetime of preparation or a moment of complete surrender. Preparation is expected by the masculine aspect of Spirit. Surrender is encouraged by the Divine Mother. How often do we trust ourselves enough to completely let go? When we can muster that much trust, the divine feminine catches and holds us. We are then launched beyond any walls we thought were there. There are bigger plans than what our fragile egos could ever anticipate.

Surrender may last only a moment or the length of our favorite karaoke track. We disappear so deeply into our groove, we become the groove itself. When our glow is witnessed, it's not only seen. It is felt. That quality is the magnetic beacon that radiates from someone who works and lives at one with their purpose.

In *The Big Leap*, Hendricks draws a direct line back to Gestalt therapy as a means of conquering fear. Fritz Perls documented decades of working with the mechanisms of the body to shift the mental experience, and vice versa. By feeling completely into whatever emotions arise, they can be transformed into something productive. Conquering fear doesn't mean not having it. It means letting it inform your path to the goal.

"There's only one way to get through the fog of fear, and that's to transform it into the clarity of exhilaration," writes Hendricks.[5] Through the lens of the 4 Permissions, the only way through the dark is to transform it into light.

Hendricks continues, "One of the greatest pieces of wisdom I've ever heard comes directly from Fritz Perls [who] said, 'Fear is excitement without the breath.'"[6] This literally means that the very same mechanisms that produce (positive) excitement also produce fear. This gives us the opportunity to directly shift fear into excitement. Just add breathing.

When we hold our breath, it's interpreted by the body as fear. We naturally seize up. As we do, we miss the opportunity the darkness is pointing to. Often, we don't even know we're getting spooked. We default to shallow breathing, or we may hold our breath completely. The mechanics of pranayama breathing, developed thousands of years ago, help draw air more deeply into the body and then forcefully release it.

This is ridiculously obvious, but breathing is a two-step process. Especially when things feel dark, we must be vigilant about exhaling. Deeply receive oxygen, nourishing every cell and capillary, and then release and expel the breath. Remember, excitement fully breathes. When you breathe through fear, your body can't tell the difference from excitement.

Conquering fear doesn't mean not having it.

It means letting it inform your path to the goal.

Standing on a quiet beach and staring out at a vast ocean can be a transcendent experience. Something about the unlimited visual distance and the rhythmic push-pull of the tides helps our worries fade into the background. The tide washes over our feet before being drawn out again. When the beach is quiet enough, and that connection deepens, our small concerns melt, and something massive seems to be breathing right alongside us. The deeper we inhale, the longer we exhale. The more we release, the more we can receive.

Imagine and eventually know your power to connect to that ocean of peace in any moment. As you exhale deeply, you release any fear, so you may receive that great light. Audacity returns.

Receive, Release, Receive, Release

Recall your Big Honkin' Dream for me. Visualize yourself being it. Living that life, achieving that thing. Awake in that dream.

Let the doubts crowd around you. Notice any apprehension.

Feel any fears that arise. This is only the murky darkness of not knowing how or when it will happen.

Take a moment to fully feel and acknowledge these feelings.

Draw your breath deep down to the base of your abdomen.

Receive fully the gift of your breath. Let it nourish you. Feel your abdomen expand to receive.

Now draw your abdomen in completely, releasing your exhale up and out.

Find the even rhythm of your breath.

In, and down (inhale). Receive.

Up, and out (exhale). Release.

Spend at least one minute in this even rhythm. Listen for the vast ocean in your breath. Now, what are your next appropriate actions toward your dream?

Do one thing.

GET UP! PERFORM ANYWAY.

———

SOMETIMES ALL the forces conspire against us, leaving us no choice. Getting up and performing anyway is one of the most valuable experiences we can have. How often do we feel fully prepared? The higher the stakes, the greater our need may be to bypass all self-doubt and throw the switch. The potential of complete failure (with witnesses) must be on the table. Being open to a public face-plant is the ultimate confrontation of our darkness. And it may help us forget the fear altogether. In many ways, it is our worst nightmare playing out in real time. Like our stress dreams of showing up to a final exam we never studied for. Buck naked. Or worse, leading a client meeting without our laptop. When there's nowhere left to hide, and the odds are so inconceivably stacked against us, we have no choice but to get on with it.

Who is the most dangerous competitor? The one with nothing to lose.

Delivering a flawless performance can be a predictable outcome of rehearsing. But it's not very rock and roll. Dancing with unforeseen chaos activates something unplanned, which makes things much more interesting. It's the dedication to constant preparation, and the willingness to cast all prep aside should the moment call for it. It's the courage to stare down a crowd of faces when we've opened ourselves to the possibility of absolute failure. We stay in it, blow by blow, embodying the ethos of the warrior—*I am open to fail, and I am willing to fight.*

Glowing or bust may look like:

*The politician who drops the politics for vulnerability.
The salesperson who relies on compelling storytelling to close the deal instead of sweating about how their slide deck isn't working. (Spoiler alert: you are the content.)
A facilitator who turns heckling from a participant into a valuable lesson for the group.
The perfect storm of public accountability and an impossible deadline, which miraculously produces our best work.*

Our surrender transforms darkness into light.
Throwing our hands up and running out of the room
isn't an option. We stay in it, and somehow something
far better happens. These are deeply uncomfortable but
necessary moments. Our biggest fears, both real and
imagined, make the perfect venue to unleash our light.

Show up like a beast
and wild rumpus in the dark

Our teenage daughter Elliott has been a professional
singer for a few years now. Last year, she woke up on
the day of a competition at the Rock and Roll Hall
of Fame unable to speak. There was no option to
reschedule. A thousand people would be in attendance,
and her band, Detention, had to deliver a fifteen-
minute showcase. Her mother and I gave Elliott a
steady cocktail of herbal remedies and medication all
day. Still, nothing more than croaks and squeaks came
out. She was understandably freaked out.

We tried vocal warm-ups. Everyone felt terrible
about the pressure she was feeling. A few minutes
before taking the stage, we committed to plan B. She
would sell the performance as an emcee, not singing
too much, just enough to win the round. "If Vince Neil
could get away with it in Mötley Crüe," I reasoned,
"then so can our kid."

Elliott quickly won over the crowd and kept the
energy up. Being fifteen years old with a rock and roll

Our biggest fears, both real and imagined, make the perfect venue **to unleash our light.**

attitude helped, because she almost seemed to make fun of her situation. Her voice was really rough, so the band stepped in to grab the focus. Fortunately, all the bands that night were having issues with their mix. Detention won the round.

Elliott's professionalism and preparation have always impressed me. And let's be honest: being a pro and being prepared are what any stage dad would harp on. Still, it's never fun to see our kids struggle. That night, though, I witnessed her full surrender to staying in the fight. In doing so, she turned the high potential for failure into her moment to glow in the dark. In the next round, she showed up like a beast and celebrated her very real joy of having a voice. Detention destroyed the Rock and Roll Hall of Fame and won the finals. Since that night, they've garnered national attention and regional airplay.

OUR GLOW ORIGINATES FROM SOMEPLACE ELSE

THE MORE I coach, the more blown away I am by the absolute singularity of each human being. We share many themes in our upbringing and education. Leaders in different industries (or countries) may share the common trappings of privilege, or the common injustices of exclusion. We share so many struggles and responsibilities, such as our relationship to time, or our instincts to provide for those we love. Even our biggest fears, and the unconscious self-defenses we use to avoid facing them, come up time and time again. These are the human parts of our human condition, the universal clown cars we learn to drive and, if we're lucky, come to love about ourselves.

Look deeper into the eyes of others and you may discover *something more* is looking back at you. When we take the time to fully connect and see others, we see beyond the two-way mirror of our common challenges. When we lose a loved one, we may feel how their neuroses and the dicey aspects of their personality passed away. At the same time, all the gifts of their being live on, spurring countless stories or the unmistakable feeling of their presence. I'm convinced that those *being* aspects of our humanity in our deepest core have never been duplicated. A vast iceberg reaching far deeper and wider than our familiar facades. No two of us share that same divine fingerprint. No two of us express it in exactly the same way. Your glow is singular to you, and the rest of us experience it whenever you're aligned from the inside out.

Our divine fingerprint in five words or less

When my team onboards a new coaching client, we get connected using a discovery process that the world-class crew at Accomplishment Coaching trained me in. It's called the Essence Conversation.[1] Distinguishing someone's Essence is at the core of ontological coaching. *Ontology* refers to "the study of being." The Essence exercise has the client briefly interview people from various areas in their lives. People who have experienced the individual over time. They ask just one question, in two parts: "What qualities do I bring into a room, [and] what shows up when I do?"

The responses that come back have undeniable themes. Many of these are obvious, while many others may be surprising, or even confronting for the recipient to hear. Every time I review the feedback, the client is stunned by the gap between their perceived gifts and how they are actually perceived by others. More proof for that piece of Southern folk wisdom: "You can't read the label from inside the jar."

Coach and client work together to chisel the emergent themes down to their roots. Essence traits are nouns, not adjectives. The final distillation of a handful of interviews, and perhaps a lifetime of relationships, comes down to five Essence words. While people may share one or two common traits, I've never seen two identical sets of five.

In the moment the client reviews their completed set, there's always a brief pause. We feel a palpable resonance in the space—an expansion. For me, it feels like coming home, back to being. This singular combination of five words is their divine fingerprint. It showed up when they did, likely at birth, and will be left behind on each of us when these bodies and egos pass on.

Facilitating the rediscovery of Essence is a sacred privilege—and one of my favorite moments in being a coach.

8 Leaders, 8 Divine Fingerprints: Their Essence

Amanda	Precision	Spark	Service	Presence	Wonder
Brendon	Service	Ease	Vision	Catalyst	Coach
Laura	Ease	Possibility	Magnetism	Power	Sobriety
Wendy	Light	Leader	Sorceress	Haven	Maestra
Kevin	Seeker	Peace	Service	Vision	Enthusiasm
Kari	Solar panel	Presence	Joy	Wonder	Passion
Robert	Openness	Leader	Connection	Safe harbor	Attunement
Mark	Presence	Seeker	Ease	Leader	Integration

Between safety and the great unknown

"At night our fear is strong," writes the youngest Nobel Prize laureate, Malala Yousafzai. "But in the morning," she continues, "in the light, we find our courage again."[2]

Glowing in the dark is working with the tension between our safety zone and the great unknown, that heavily guarded border between the edge of our safety and the edge of our dream, where we tend to freeze up. We'll find that tension whenever we're working toward anything we haven't done before—and in far less sexy moments, like when giving or receiving

Your glow is singular to you, and the rest of us experience it whenever you're aligned from the inside out.

feedback. When we're confronted by the prospect of our growth and expansion, we retreat. We also hit that upper limit, going psycho-kitty when we can't handle the tasty goodness we're creating. Acknowledging our fear doesn't make us weak. It makes us human beings who care.

When we don't consciously acknowledge and work with our fear (the dark), we forfeit our light and retreat back to the status quo.

However, when we stay in the fear long enough and let it inform us, we can summon the lightning. We reclaim our power to convert fear into fuel, into excitement, and ignite uncertainty into possibility.

The first mask to dissolve is Phantom Pest. We step out of our darkness to claim our power. The bombastic lightning in *Thor: Ragnarok* (with blaring Led Zeppelin) comes to mind. We also move beyond our anxieties of clock-time. In our full expression, the moment expands to make room. Speedy Rabbit slows the hell down and fades away. Because we have cultivated the meditation habit, we've grown more comfortable with being with what is. As we get up to perform, despite the depths of our greatest fears, we feel every emotion that comes up. We feel into each, receiving grace and guidance. Game Face cracks down the center and shatters away. Our unfiltered, authentic smile returns. All that's left is Essence. All we're left with is light.

Glowing in the dark is the work of being a patient warrior for our gifts. Our light is the medicine our aching planet needs. We all know it. Rather than staying hidden or plowing through by trial and error, take some space to relax. Feel any and all resistance. Work with the darkness. Reclaim your God-given permission to glow.

EXPAND
YOUR AWARENESS

What is one quality that you could bring into any space?

Hints: People have consistently thanked you for it. It's a noun, not an adjective.

Come in little dark satellite

Just before the great COVID-19 shutdown of 2020, I was running to the airport for a flight to Costa Rica. My team and I were hosting our This Epic Life retreat just under the wire. A couple of short weeks later, everything would be closed. I had been writing a song for our guests. Sharing my childhood dreams and my early career as a touring musician and songwriter is a fun, if not terrifying, perk of my job. My harmonium travels with me for chants before and after morning meditation.

Glowing in the dark is the work of being a patient warrior for our gifts. **Our light is the medicine our aching planet needs.**

The guitar comes along for energy breaks and comic relief. Sometimes we'll break into hours of 1980s sing-alongs or guilty pleasures from the nineties. This isn't your standard retreat with eye gazing and singing bowls. Music is my way to call people out to play. To give us all permission.

I approach songwriting like solving a mystical puzzle. In the dark. Some songs arrive easily, and others have taken years to wrestle into submission. The road littered with the landmines of perfectionism and fear. Other songs, like the one below, arrive in a couple of hours. This is how I know the 4 Permissions are yoga. "Union with Spirit," however we interpret that, is a blooming vine that propagates throughout our lives. Each of the permissions has arrived at the time I needed it. For many years, there was one. Then two. Three, now four. If you told me just six years ago that my job would be to gather world-class leaders together in a place like Costa Rica or Encinitas, and then sing them a song I wrote about four permissions, I would have laughed. Then I would have actually thought about it. "Oooohhh, that actually sounds kickass. Do tell me more!"

I share this to illustrate, once again, that glowing in the dark looks different for each of us. No one knows what your full glow will look or sound like. We feel its warmth when it lights up the space. Full self-expression is as unique as trillions of falling snowflakes. As nuanced as nearly eight billion divine fingerprints.

These lyrics may provide a summary of our journey together thus far. They also set the stage for the 4th Permission. If you'd like to hear the full track, please visit ThisEpicLife.com/music.

In the Light

When did we fall out of orbit?
Circling around the night
When our skin wears thin,
  we forget where we've been
Come in little dark satellite
Rest, rest, rest
Feel all there is to feel
You will glow, glow again
  as you heal
No matter how long you've been waiting
You're never quite ready for Grace
She cuts cloudy skies,
  pours in the skylights
Kneels down to kiss your face
Saying rest, rest, rest
And feel, all there is to feel
You will glow, glow again
  as you heal
Now we're running on stage at the edge of the dream
Feeling unprepared, but ready to scream
I will glow, you will glow, we all glow in the dark
I've watched you prepare for this all of your life
  and you're open to fail, but willing to fight
I will glow, you will glow, we'll all glow in the light

Remind me there's two kinds of fire
Remind me the danger is real
While one fire forges, the other consumes
Leaving dust, of what could've been steel
We'll rest, rest, rest
    and feel while we can still feel
We'll glow, glow again as we heal
Now we're running on stage, wide awake in the dream
Feeling unprepared, and ready to scream
I will glow, you will glow, we all glow in the dark
We've been preparing all of our lives
We're open to fail, but willing to fight
I will glow, you will glow, we'll all glow in the light
In the light.

Awareness + Practice =
PERMISSION TO GLOW
IN THE DARK

1　**In your journal, answer each of the Expand Your Awareness prompts in this section.**

2　List all your weekly tasks that are energy-depleting. Outsource them, or reduce your time spent on them by 25 percent minimum. Whenever you catch yourself doing a crappy task (like editing your own podcast), think of the Meatloaf song "I'd Do Anything for Love (But I Won't Do That)"! Better yet, watch the tedious almost-eight-minute music video every time you regress.

3　Identify the aspects of your life right now that overlap with your Big Honkin' Dream. Who are you already being to create that new reality?

4　Write a short list of the predictable forces that stop you. Beside each, note which aspect of yourself this force cuts you off from loving. Next, cross each item out and write next to it, "I completely love and accept myself now."

5　Empower your Essence. Explore ontological coaching and hire someone who fully sees your untapped potential. Surrender into the process and work hard to maximize the value.

6   Write a short paragraph on what glowing in the dark looks like for you. In your full expression. In your relationships. In your career. Your Big Honkin' Dream.

7   Throw the switch and perform anyway. What magical creation have you been delaying? Practice the "Release, Receive" process in this section. Begin.

Permission 4 is the power of the collective. It is the accumulated light of leaders and organizations that have done the work of glowing in the dark. It is symbolized by a family of lighthouses, each unobstructed by the others' abilities to do their jobs. Cooperation and collaboration are our highest aspects—and will solve our greatest challenges.

PERMISSION 4

PERMISSION TO GLOW IN THE LIGHT

LIGHTHOUSE SYMBOLOGY

THE LIGHTHOUSE symbolizes the dignity of service. Technology may render lighthouses obsolete. Still, our shorelines will remain dotted with rotating beacons.

From a sailor's perspective, the lighthouse is the first sign of home. Standing alone in the dark fog, like your mom waiting up. Before we took to the skies, we took to the seas. Lighthouses were the porchlights of the motherland. Now, on our Google Earth, with precise coordinates bouncing off countless satellites, what purpose could an old concrete tower serve? The purpose of a lighthouse has evolved, from the practical to the spiritual.

The lighthouse is the embodiment of selfless leadership. It's some kind of fierce love to stare down any storm blowing in. The patience to hold vigil until the sun comes up. Because the sun always, eventually comes up. The beacon holds light in the sky. *God forbid, if even one doesn't return, I'll scan every black horizon for eternity.* Someone with beacon magnetism will never be forgotten. They draw all resources and allies. Their evolution outgrew "Look at me" and replaced it with "Look at you" and "How can I help?"

The fourth permission begins with the solo practitioner who has devoted themselves to glowing in the dark. Their example calls others, but not just anyone, forward. A beacon attracts a diversity of beacons in their own right. Counterparts in their willingness to give and receive. Their radiance draws others who've grown bored with conformity and competition.

Cooperation has always been in the divine plan. It doesn't matter how far the real world is from achieving it, or how Shangri-la it sounds. We are the ones who chose to build lighthouses far apart from one another. Our ailing planet demands radical cooperation and acts of service. Cooperation deepens into collaboration, the melting pot of freedom. Towers of varying heights, colors, and patterns all willing to glow.

We are strengthened by our diversity and unstoppable when we collaborate. A grid of lighthouses. We experience our potential only when we drop the doom loops of comparison and scarcity.

We give more light as we receive more support. "We got this" looks like an integrated grid of lighthouses, willing to serve while staying open to receive.

Darkness optional, designed to shine 24-7, even on the brightest days.

The lighthouse, in being our fiercest ally, inspires us to be a fierce ally to all—to give ourselves and everyone Permission to Glow in the Light.

INVOCATION

As one glows, many will glow.

Our full expression attracts compatible souls who form an interconnected grid of light.

The upliftment of our planet will be realized on the collective level.

Our human family unleashes Spirit when we operate as one integrated system.

I release "I got this" and receive "We got this."

I give myself—and the entirety of our human family—

Permission to Glow in the Light.

WHAT HAVE YOU BEEN PREPARING FOR?

F OR YEARS, I incorrectly assumed that glowing in the dark was enough. Our journeys were complete once we found full expression.

Expansion would continue indefinitely by cycling through Permissions 1 through 3: chill, feel, glow. Rinse, repeat.

Life has this funny way of tossing us off the mechanical bull once we figure out how to mount it. So, we quiet ourselves down again, feel into new marching orders, and find our glow through the darkness. Noble work. And a bit hamster wheel–ish. Which could easily get hacked by the ego. Assuming that expansion begins and ends with us reinforces the rah-rah for achievement touted by personal-development cassettes from the eighties.

I call this affliction "I got this." It's everywhere. Side effects include corny mantras like, "If it is to be, it's up to me," or telling everyone, "You got this!" all the time. LinkedIn could make those three words one of their autofill responses, if it hasn't already. "I got this" is usually mistaken for confidence. We learned that "I got this" implies adding value. Too often, I see it limiting far more value than it creates. It's a subtle to overt form of power-hoarding. "I got this" is quality control for the untrusting achiever.

Rock "I got this!" a little too hard, and you'll awaken the fourth frenemy within. This default is a vacuous mass called Dark Star. At first, "I got this" has the energy of the 1988 Crystal Light National Aerobics Championship (absolutely worth YouTubing the opening dance number). We take on a little too much, and we incorrectly assume that because we're handling it, we must be doing it better than anyone else could have. Our Phantom Pest hides in busy work. Left unchecked, Dark Star assumes control.

Dark Star guards one of the final frontiers of personal growth. It's a default way of being that *keeps us from receiving help*. We get so good at managing outcomes that we get by without letting others assist. The work gets done. Success happens. Yet meaning and fulfillment can't be found without trust. Connection feels nonexistent. Dark Star has created such a ridiculously safe distance from the risk of being let down by others. Dark Star may say they're holding space for everyone. They may be universally adored. But in refusing to fully trust their team or be coachable, their safe distance is felt as a chilling void. Inaccessible. A great deflector who trains us to eventually stop offering help.

Most Dark Stars are unaware they are even doing this. Others may be well aware, resigned to the immense untapped potential they're leaving on the table. Dark Star may suffer in the open by throwing tantrums when anyone predictably screws up. Often, though, they suffer in silence at the far end of the galaxy, their Game Face pleasantly requesting status updates while everything mysteriously continues to suck.

EXPAND
YOUR AWARENESS

In what ways do you hold yourself apart from receiving help?

Where is your line between what you're able to receive and what you're not?

How do you grade your abilities to fully receive and give?

Awakening to our vocation has never been about just us. Meaning is realized in serving the universal good.

Has it ever really been about us?

Awakening to our vocation has never been about just us. Meaning is realized in serving the universal good. Service is so much more than good business or the right thing to do. If we believe in an Organizing Consciousness, we need to consider the goals it may have for us. A strong body and an overflowing bank account are goals we create. Meanwhile, in every direction and in any community, we can see the harsh realities of VUCA. Climate change, racism, famine, conspiracy theories, and blatant hostility replacing civil discourse are just a few views from any window. All are symptoms of a world struggling with relentless change.

Is becoming our fully expressed selves enough to make progress on any one of these urgent issues? Certainly, it is. We have a greater capacity to serve when we are at peace. We emanate that peace to others. Our peace is added to the collective ocean of consciousness. That was part of the divine plan. Turbulent waves of change have been preparing us. Tumbled and tossed, our sharp edges eventually become ground down into smooth sea glass. We start by no longer being part of the problem. But to be part of the solution, we learn to selflessly give our light. We help curb injustice. Finding our glow is the medicine the world has been aching for.

There's never a comfy time to step beyond "What about me?" or "I got this." We're reminded every day that the world needs more from us. Many career execs eventually find themselves at an existential fork in the road. They're more qualified to lead than ever, but constant change eventually makes their big salaries unsustainable. Their choice is either to retire (and figure out how to *not* drive their spouse crazy) or find a new, better way to serve. Deciding to go it alone (Dark Star) or creating a new career isn't easy. Every frenemy within will come out to play. An executive is used to having support teams to drive their agenda.

If there's grace to be found in the screeching jungle of career reinvention, it's in service to others. Almost every action, minute to minute, requires us to not make everything about us. As we surrender into serving the greater good, we gain deeper perceptions from our meditation practice. Early in our Permission to Chill, we only showed up to receive some calm. We demanded a pause. We expected results. Less stress. A bit further down the path, our attachments loosen, then fall away. Something shifts. We learn to care less about what we get from sitting still. Our investment becomes about *what we can give.*

Permission to Glow in the Light is selfless service for the universal good. It's the redistribution of our light toward the survival and well-being of others. The round-the-back route to self-realization through complete surrender to "We got this." The simultaneous giving and receiving of help, healing, and light. Like a solar panel inside a tanning bed powered by solar panels. Our glow, releasing any sense of self, burns solely to benefit others. Our darkness is laid bare before billions of healing beacons. Small concerns of "What about me?" melt before the collective concern: "What about us?" The fourth permission has been called seva yoga. *Seva* means "selfless service" in Sanskrit. When you perform seva yoga, you renounce your own selfish desires and instead give your time and energy to the greater good.[1]

> *Stacey Abrams exemplifies Permission 4, turning a campaign loss into a win for Black voters and for our democracy.*

> *Scott Harrison's leadership with Charity: Water continues its quest to solve the world's water crisis in our lifetime.*

> *Alex Schulze and Andrew Cooper founded 4Ocean in 2017, and by selling goods made from recycled plastic, they have removed tens of millions of pounds of plastic from the world's oceans.*

These examples may seem large in scale. In each case, upliftment occurs with the fierce vision and commitment of the leader and it can't be accomplished alone. Start where you are. Chances are our communities have countless opportunities to align our work with real, positive impact. Union with Spirit through service. Our capacity to receive expands exponentially in our capacity to give.

Humans have become effective and efficient at making gigantic messes. With pressing urgency and harrowing consequences. At the core of every reckoning we face is the darkness of fear and greed. Permission to Glow in the Light assumes greater responsibility for our actions, and for our planet. It takes power and audacity to acknowledge our universal suffering while assuming responsibility for our collective healing. We can pray to be rescued from the mess we've created. And in meditation we may hear the response: "God sent help. She sent you."

Daya Mata, born Rachel Faye Wright in 1914, was the first female leader of a global spiritual organization, Self-Realization Fellowship. She served as president and sanghamata (mother of the congregation) from 1955 to 2010. Her words hit with perfect timing just now. She speaks from direct perception of the profound truths she learned from her teacher, or guru, Paramahansa Yogananda:

> As we go meditating deeper and deeper, the consciousness begins to expand. There awakens a longing to forget this little fleshly form and behold the Self in all beings. We want to do for others; the desire to selflessly serve mankind.[2]

Embodying all 4 Permissions in leadership

David Bishop is someone who embodies all four permissions. He's the former head of Sony Pictures and, prior to that, Metro-Goldwyn-Mayer (MGM) Home Entertainment.

Our glow, releasing any sense of self, burns solely to benefit others. **Our darkness is laid bare before billions of healing beacons.**

Early in my career, I worked many levels beneath David at MGM. I recall his leadership being very culture-focused and (before we had a name for it) high EQ. He led in times of crisis, during and after September 11, and in times of major growth, from $300 million to over $1 billion in gross revenue.

David went on to lead home entertainment for Sony Pictures, where his team contributed over $20 billion in revenue through a recession. He mobilized the industry to develop the Blu-ray and digital distribution formats, innovations that got him inducted into the *Variety Magazine* Hall of Fame.

David earned a comfortable retirement, but instead he channeled his experience into service. He completed a graduate certificate in organizational coaching and now coaches a new generation of leaders. He also discovered a passion for ending hunger. He devotes a ton of time and energy to raising awareness and money to fight food insecurity. He is the founder and chairman of Fast Forward to End Hunger and has served as chairman for the Los Angeles Regional Food Bank.

And the light keeps coming. I remember David's band of industry vets rocking out during company conferences. He would get up and perform "Secret Agent Man." He's a serious singer and guitarist. We caught up last year, and he shared an incredible milestone. He casually mentioned he has been practicing transcendental meditation twice daily. For more than forty-five years.

I literally can't think of anyone better equipped to prepare leaders. Rather than letting David's accomplishments intimidate you, look deeper at the steady build. The results of a lifetime of giving time. Service, like meditation, is a consistent drop of water that will eventually cut through granite. All 4 Permissions are invitations to keep showing up. Dude is chill. He speaks and coaches on emotional intelligence. Glows on the mic, glows in the light. *Chill, feel, glow, serve.* Rinse, repeat.

EXPAND
YOUR AWARENESS

What selfless act of service could you offer the world?

(Don't worry: you may already be getting paid for it.)

WE ARE ONE OF MANY

A FEW YEARS ago, I supported my first retreat in Costa Rica. The event was organized by my friend (and *menschtor*) Jonathan Fields of Good Life Project. I had been a participant a couple of years earlier and was now given the opportunity to teach and help design the experience. These were my first, humbling attempts at leading group meditation. Although I had all the struggles of a novice teacher, something felt oddly familiar. Two of Jonathan's many gifts are to see deeply into what people are here to express and then to provide the community and connection to express it.

On our final morning, my friend Scotty led a silent, mindful walk through the coffee plantation across the street. I caught up to the group as the sun rose over the hill. Sunlight poured like streams through endless rows of bright green arabica plants. It was the dry season, and the sky was clear. We all had sunglasses on, which further insulated our silent, individual experiences. We were awake in the predawn as the plantation and surrounding jungle came to life. Everything felt elevated. It had already been a spiritual experience. Now, there was a palpable vibe of connection with one another, the moment we were in, and this holy ground.

This is one of the miracles of retreats. Our bonds were forged largely in silence. I can still see vividly each of the thirty-five people present for that moment. We all flew in alone, shuttled up there as strangers, and left as lifelong allies. Costa Rica was expanding our capacity for connection. The expansiveness we felt was almost overwhelming. New relationships opened doors of possibility. Through the challenging and transformational years that lay just ahead of me, many of these same souls reappeared as teammates, coaches, clients, and family.

I fell back to the rear of the procession.

Months earlier, I had started writing a song that I planned to share with the group later that evening. The final verse was still tormenting me, until this perfectly quiet moment of connection. Solving the word puzzle was silenced by truth:

What if I'm only one—of many?
And there are others out there who've been waiting
for me?

Our grid of blinding light stretches worldwide
as one we rise, as one we shine

That morning planted a seed.

Permissions 1 to 3 are anything but selfish. Light amplifies light. Permission 4 is a team sport. Connection with others is the venue of giving and receiving. Connection is the conquest and the reward. All our individual work is in preparation to assemble into a unified whole. Our lives are spent pursuing deeper connections. To self, to others, to All That Is.

Expanding the light out and out and out

Two remarkable women sharpened my perception of the fourth permission. The first was Laura Neff, an outstanding coach. Laura messaged one morning, overflowing with all the feels and possibilities. Her insight was that somehow glowing in the dark didn't quite feel sufficient. "What if all limits were removed? What if we could unapologetically stand and glow in our own *light*?" All I could do was respond like a *Bill and Ted's*–era Keanu Reeves: "Whoa."

A year later, I was interviewing my friend and superheroine Ani DiFranco for my podcast. Her family was passing through Akron on vacation, so we grabbed time for an in-person interview. In many moments, I literally couldn't believe Ani was really kicking it barefoot in my office, answering all my fanatical-nerd questions about her memoir, *No Walls and the Recurring Dream*.

All our individual work is in preparation to **assemble into a unified whole.**

We explored her decades lived under stage lights. That time she felt completely unprepared to jam with Prince. A powerful opening of love and wisdom came pouring in. She was telling a story about folk legend Pete Seeger, and I felt the heartbreaking beauty from a lifetime of unwavering feminism and activism. Ani shared that after Pete Seeger received one of his many lifetime-achievement awards, a reporter asked what accomplishment he was most proud of in his ninety-plus years.

Pete paused, then said: "I stayed married to the best woman I ever met. And we had four children and six grandchildren." Ani got choked up. When I asked what the emotion was, she said: "That's the hard shit. Loving each other. It's what we're all out there failing at."

She continued: "I thought it was a powerful, beautiful thing for a man of such accomplishment, who is held in such high esteem, to bodycheck that perspective of success and just bring it right back down. Well, what if success is loving each other? Especially to do it like he did, which is to expand it out, and out, and out. Because that's the hard shit."

Another songwriter and activist wrote a mantra that shakes me every time I hear it:

"I am, you are, we are enough."

In seven words, Angie Haze captures the profound hardships of exclusion. Also, how acceptance rises to meet any challenge. Loving ourselves and one another is like meditating daily, staying sober, or pursuing conscious leadership. If it were easy, everyone would be doing it.

Assemble the grid: Integration

Integration is the assembly of various pieces into a unified whole. In learning and development, integration is the accumulation of knowledge and the digestion of it into wisdom.

In our high-VUCA world, integration creates space. First, we integrate ourselves. Only then can our glow merge with others'. If we can't be with our inner chaos, we'll never find the strength to give selflessly. As we discover ways to be with the suffering of others, we receive the gifts of being human. We discover how to participate in our much-needed healing.

My own experiments in personal growth have been to integrate the seemingly disparate aspects of my life while coaching others to do the same. We experience peace and flow when our sacred life ingredients aren't in a constant battle royal. There is creativity and freedom in learning to integrate our soul with our work, our family with our art, or our vitality with our leadership.

Marc Blaushild is the president and CEO of Famous Supply, a fourth-generation family business with nearly a thousand associates in forty locations. Marc's personal calendar is a color-coded masterpiece of what we call "integration points" and non-negotiables. At a glance, he can scan the 11-by-17 calendar and see a year full of family time, golf tournaments, epic vacations, and all of his biggest business priorities, including giving back. His right-hand woman, Julie, keeps his schedule optimized to be energizing. The rest is delegated. In one of his offices, he has a standing desk attached to a treadmill.[1]

Every area of our life deserves its own type of focus, but at the end of the day, there's still only one of us. Depletion happens when we assume there's not enough of us to go around. By integration, we bend the rigidity of clock-time. We become simultaneously all of the above, yet none of the above. We are unattached and not limited to the label in any one area. Permissions 1 to 3 are the work of the integrated soul. We chill, feel, and glow to exit our personal crazy train, as we assume full responsibility for who we are.

In giving ourselves the permissions repeatedly, we realize, *I am whole*. The greatest gift is when we realize we are *one of many*. We have never been alone. We've been prepared to integrate into a larger system. There is no threat to our sense of wholeness. We are able to give and receive in infinite capacity.

A grid gives more power than the sum of its individual bulbs. We see the spectrum of our collective potential like a 4K ultra-HD image, once we lose awareness of any single pixel. All along, it's been the destiny of the sole little glow lamp to surrender selflessly into the greater good. Permission to Glow in the Light is the power of the integrated collective. How else could we even attempt to face our collective darkness?

On my desk stands a legendary defender of the universe. Fellow Gen Xers may remember a cartoon called *Voltron* from 1984. (I'm breaking the only rule of Gen X: never admit you belong to Gen X or ask any member to identify as such.) Voltron was a giant, badass robot formed by five separate robotic lions.

Each lion had its own special power. Every episode, some new alien threat beat up the lions to the point when they had to say: "Okay, enough of this crap. We're forming Voltron."

You could count on Voltron to whoop intergalactic ass and restore peace to the universe. My desk Voltron reminds me of the power of integration. It's built from my other favorite integrated system, Lego. Our family of five spent an entire day, each of us building one of the five lions. Late that night, my son, Leon, and I formed Voltron. Our giddy power surge felt like Thanos snapping the Infinity Stones.

There's no challenge that our singular glow, when integrated into the glow of others, cannot face. We're unconscious while wreaking havoc in our own lives, and in all lives around our planet. We justify our actions with greed and fear. The consciousness we find in the first three permissions compounds in the fourth. In our collective light, we'll see where the solutions are. Find the patience. Find the courage to endure, protect, and uplift. The audacity to love one another.

What other choice do we have than to be that brave?

Permission to Glow in the Light is the **power of the integrated collective.**

Billions upon billions of flickering little pixels think they're doing what they need to do to survive. Inadvertently, we're messing up a lot of stuff. How many grids of light will our redemption take? Who does humankind get to become as we rise to meet so many formidable threats?

A central theme of the *Bhagavad Gita*, the Hindu scripture extolling yoga, is that God's great game was designed so we may reclaim our consciousness. The game of life encourages us to wake up and remind ourselves through practice that we are all-powerful extensions of God's great light. And in union with all other extensions of that great light, nothing is unconquerable.

We got this.

EXPAND
YOUR AWARENESS

What areas of your life can be integrated into the whole of you?

What communities would benefit from your integration?

How are you willing to serve?

FINDING THE LIGHT, AND HOW TO GLOW IN IT

THE LIGHT pulls us into it. Often mistaken for darkness, new threats can strike like lightning. Our natural tendency may be to deny what we see. We assume it's too painful to deal with. Ignored, the fires spread. We can look back on how we handled (or didn't handle) the early weeks of the COVID-19 pandemic. There were the tactical concerns of how to physically distance and whether or not to wear masks. Fear of the unknown became a constant, like a persistent, heavy static.

As the months and potentially years roll on, we just want it to end. Feeling we have no personal power to improve the situation, we may defer to some leader or vaccine to save us. But nothing drastically improves, at least not right away. We can see the vast range of human responses to the uncertainty the virus has created. From denial to cynicism to absurdity and beyond. We become wary of even wrapping our head around the current stats: millions of deaths worldwide and climbing. Many of our favorite businesses closed for good. Aspects of how we lived changed forever.

The light is where we look for it

In her classic book *When Things Fall Apart*, Buddhist nun and teacher Pema Chödrön captures the essence of our physical world as a spiritual classroom: "Nothing ever goes away until it has taught us what we need to know."[1] Wherever you stand on wearing masks or an issue like climate change, you're still being asked to adapt to their effects. When the world eventually finds its new normal, we can ask, what was this virus here to teach us? If we resonate with Pema's wisdom, what do we need to learn that would make it go away?

The light from this particular darkness comes in a tediously slow drip. The gifts of boredom. Time to create. Countless opportunities to think first of others who may be at higher risk than us. The courtesy of not putting our spring break plans ahead of the well-being of the whole. An abundance of time with our families, which gives us more quality time if we're lucky. In the first month, I learned that the mountains beyond Los Angeles and urban India could be seen if we drove less for even a couple of weeks. The cruise-ship polluted waters off the Florida Keys recovered while we stayed home.

Then came the rapid development of vaccines with promising results. Creative distribution through supply chains; shots administered in stadiums. More people than ever stepping up to play a role in the recovery. More time to be more grateful for all the little things. Craving hugs, human contact. Every moment we choose to be grateful over settling for boredom.

If there's a gift in adapting to a global pandemic, it could be that we're living more in line with our values. Fewer dress slacks, more Zoom calls. Fewer pointless meetings, and way more intention. Less gluttony in entertaining ourselves, more meaningful time with people we love. Supporting one another through something that was as uncomfortable as it was unprecedented.

We find the light whenever and wherever we consciously look for it. Darkness, of course, works in exactly the same way. It results in more suffering and isolation, if that's the look you're going for. A simple way to summon the light is by mentally or verbally chanting a mantra. We can prime our minds to find connection, to be grateful.

The light around us and within us

One of Paramahansa Yogananda's metaphysical meditations is a perfect reminder of the light around us and within us. Close your eyes and take some deep, nourishing breaths. Mentally repeat to yourself:

I am submerged in eternal light.
It permeates every particle of my being.
I am living in that light.
The Divine Spirit fills me within, and without.[2]

There's no improving upon anything the guru offers; however, we may notice an expansiveness in widening the circle:

We are submerged in eternal light.
It permeates every particle of our being.
We are living in that light.
The Divine Spirit fills us within, and without.

A consistent truth arises. Whether we're glowing in our light or shuddering from the enormities of our darkness, *we're all in this together*.

THE MEASURE OF A LEADER

A S MENTIONED early on, leading others is not limited to your day job. Leadership is a way of being. I hope you've realized how crucial your role is to the well-being of the planet.

The measure of a leader is their capacity to develop others and let them lead. In surrounding themselves with high-caliber people, they find increasing levels of satisfaction and impact. Their glow isn't diminished by others. They are happy to give full credit to their team as their focus widens to other areas. Their greatest contribution is to foster high levels of collaboration.

The biggest opportunity (and potential threat) to the success of the team is the confidence of the leader. When we slip back into "I got this" behavior, the need

The measure of a leader is their capacity to develop others and let them lead.

for control tightens. Things slow down. In worrying about ourselves, we shut out the light of the greater good. In contrast, we can empower others much more capable than ourselves. Eventually, we won't confuse our value with what got done today. Our contribution is evaluated on the diversity of people we've brought together and our ability to navigate unforeseen challenges.

Conscious leaders aren't interested in any hierarchical gap between themselves and their team. They maintain presence. Their personal power (glow) is a ubiquitous force for good that others draw from. They stand shoulder to shoulder with those they lead. When it comes to their vision, they stay elevated. *Projects need to be managed. People deserve to be led.*

EXPAND
YOUR AWARENESS

If you had to write and live by a two-sentence definition of leadership, what would it be?

Great leadership is catalytic and magnetic

Great leadership inspires us to get moving and stay that way until we're past the goal. Permission to Glow in the Dark helped us rise through the ranks to assume some level of leadership. We tapped our strengths and focused our talents on being in service of others. Permission to Glow in the Light is our opportunity to deepen the experience for everyone.

Our work now includes paying forward the permission to glow that we give ourselves. By doing so, we're encouraging others to shine in their unique ways, while unlocking our capacity to glow as a collective.

Permission to glow in action means:

Acknowledge Essence to Essence
Focus less on a teammate's tactical accomplishments. Instead, publicly thank them for the being they brought to the project. Share what you learn from how they show up.

Focus less on how others deliver
Share why a task or deliverable is important. Agree on what it might look like and when it's due. Then leave the "how" completely up to them. Affirm their commitment and the spirit they bring to it.

Celebrate diversity in all people and perspectives
Admit things like, "I never would have thought of that." Defer to them: "What do you think?"

Make well-being a perennial obsession

Intend to always leave people 200 percent better than when they found you. Not just better at their job. Better human beings. Better connected to self, others, and All That Is.

Give less advice, more coaching

Michael Bungay Stanier's stellar books The Coaching Habit *and* The Advice Trap *are constant inspirations and recommendations for leaders wanting to unlock the potential of their people.*[1]

Will leading others include plenty of disagreements and feedback? Those are a given. Days may seem busy, with new challenges arising constantly for us and our teams. Don't let the work stuff overshadow what a privilege it is to serve and lead.

Trust that as we practice the 4 Permissions we'll find greater capacity and adaptability. Time will expand to allow for deeper connection. From our space of *chill*, and in our ability to navigate our *feels*, we will be more than capable of navigating toward the light—whatever the journey demands of us.

Awareness + Practice =
PERMISSION TO GLOW
IN THE LIGHT

1   **In your journal, answer each of the Expand Your Awareness prompts in this section.**

2   Look objectively at your current role. What (or who) is your work in service of? Can your work be aligned with the greater good?

3   If you have direct reports, reinvent your 1:1 meeting structure. Base it on what best serves them. Whatever time you have together, make 80 percent of it about being, connection, and coaching. The remaining 20 percent is more than enough for project updates.

4   Shift your relationship to your team. What if you actually don't have a VP, manager, or direct reports? What if you're a team, and your job is to serve as you would your number-one favorite client?

5   Meditate and reflect on your leadership journey. Whom do you influence, and whom do you lead? What's your ideal seat on the bus?

Positive, lasting change requires more than wanting things to be different. It takes a lot of showing up and occasionally hard work. Change has a shot of sticking when we play it as a game. Self-compassion is crucial. It's okay to start small. We'll activate the permissions as we apply what we've learned.

THE
MECHANICS OF
COMPASSIONATE
CHANGE

ACCEPT WHERE YOUR JOURNEY BEGINS

WHEN IT comes to activating permissions and unleashing all possibilities, you can begin only from where you are. Each of the permissions is a path from panic to peace to power to eventual transcendence. The first step is to orient yourself to where you are in that journey. Every location up and down the path will either challenge or inspire you to go further.

Much of my personal and professional life has been dedicated to forming daily practices. Positive, lasting change begins and ends with self-compassion. We waste so much time bellyaching about where we should be on any path. There was a time, young reader, when MTV played music videos, and the worst things you could be considered were a poser or a hack. These four paths can't be faked or hacked. More like lovingly tended to and enjoyed. My hope is you'll find wonder and reverence wherever you begin. And if we're being honest, we'll still off-road and party with our frenemies from time to time.

Each of the 4 Permissions warrants its own book. What follows are the 7 Compassionate Laws of Personal Change. These are your points of departure for activating and living the 4 Permissions. Pro tip: Kick off this journey with the powerful activation process below and then complete the practice sections that close each of the permissions sections. You will be drawn to the right resources, teachers, and venues for transformation. Your road will rise to meet you. If you do nothing more than empower these 7 Compassionate Laws of Personal Change, you will experience profound shifts throughout your life.

Trust the process
(and I won't waste your time)

Some years ago, I worked in education and development for an ad tech company. My job required experimenting with countless ways to engage adult learners. Their time and attention was ridiculously

Positive, lasting change begins and ends with self-compassion.

expensive. Wasting it wasn't an option. When I pulled a hundred sellers out of their markets to train up some new skill, you could feel the discontent of the overcaffeinated, Game Face-rocking Speedy Rabbits in the room.

Executive coaching provided the lab to test and refine these approaches. Each week, including the one we're in, my active clients and I are applying these principles. We are all giving it our best shots to adapt to change and reclaim our power.

For most of us, giving ourselves permission isn't a one-and-done event. Permission takes root over time through practice. If you find that hard to accept, please revisit Permission 1: Permission to Chill (the hell out). It's not practice itself that sucks, necessarily. It's our *relationship* to practicing that encourages either progress or the unhealthy story that keeps us making excuses.

This last part of the book is organized to demystify the process of getting started, and to make the journey expansive and fun.

PERMISSION TO SUCK (FOR JUST A BIT)

J
UST BECAUSE you're the most chill, glowing unicorn we know, it doesn't mean you can skip these steps. Everyone starts at zero. This should be liberating. If you've taken a psychology class, you may recall the four stages of competence, sometimes referred to as the conscious competence learning model.[1] It identifies four psychological states we move through as we develop a new skill. In adopting any new behavior or habit, we start in the dark, and move toward the light.

We begin in unconscious incompetence *(I told you it was dark in there).*
As we find our footing, we move up to conscious incompetence. Or, as I call it, The Desert. We are well aware of how terrible we are at this skill.
Perhaps by Grace, we eventually ascend to conscious competence.
But we're not done yet. Ultimately, we're after unconscious competence, when we're no longer consciously performing the new skill.

We need to make peace with the second level here. Crossing the desert of conscious incompetence sucks. This nude sprint through the cold cafeteria of personal growth is when people throw up their hands and quit. We get so used to performing well that tolerating anything less feels like a waste of time.

It is frustrating to create so much awareness about how terrible we are. When we first meditate, we wonder if the silence just turns up the volume on our inner critic. Think of the years wandering in the dark, not knowing or caring that you didn't have the skills.

Turn up the self-compassion. Be more like the determined, happy toddler figuring out how to walk, and less like the jaded bureaucrat, arms folded in "I got this" position.

What is the easiest way to get the motivation train rolling? *Design a game you will win.* Give yourself the gift of temporary, maximum suckage. Put all your focus on consistency, as we discussed in Permission 1. Consistency is everything at this tender stage.

THE 7 (COMPASSIONATE) LAWS OF PERSONAL CHANGE

T HESE SEVEN laws have been used to quit everything from alcohol to caffeine to overspending.
They have guided us to create countless healthy
habits, write books (like this one), and transform
many marriages and careers.

1 **Activate your commitment**
This is our soul-level reminder of how bad we really
want it.

2 **Declare and fulfill**

For the next twenty to thirty days, what will you do, and by when? Be specific and realistic. You're unlikely to meditate four hours a day. What is a game you can win? *I will meditate for five to ten minutes a day for thirty days*, or *I will meditate for ten minutes a minimum of four days per week.*

3 **Start small**

Embrace your humble beginnings.

4 **Choose consistency over duration**

Ancient Roman poet Ovid coined the phrase *Gutta cavat lapidem, non vi sed saepe cadendo*, which translates to "A water drop hollows a stone, not by force, but by falling often."[1] Release attachment to how long you practice. Maintain relentless consistency. It could take as little as five minutes, but you must honor your commitment daily. No matter what. What's the minimum commitment you will honor consistently?

5 **Celebrate and savor**

Throw yourself a small, regular love fest. Savor the tiniest benefits.

6 **When you fail, just get back up**

Should you miss a day, quietly recommit. Consistency begins again tomorrow, or better yet right now.

7 **Deepen, expand**
There are no limits to the benefits you will experience. Always go deeper and expand your practice as it expands you. Meditating last week doesn't make you a meditator. Showing up for years and decades does. Devotion awakens *Spirit*.

Notice how *easy on you* these laws appear. Learning anything new is hard enough, let alone mastering it. We naturally resist anything that feels hammered into us. By contrast, we'll embrace anything that feeds our sense of *progressive realization*. Compassion at every step. Are you ready?

1. Activate your commitment

This book up to now—and your entire journey that brought you here—has been preparing you for this moment. Without a commitment to a desired change, we won't maintain the focus and perseverance we need. Commitments can live inside our hearts, but they are much more powerful when written down. A commitment is not one time only. It is more like year twenty-five of a marriage than your wedding day.

Don't be a member of the Speedy Rabbit majority. It's too obvious (yawn) that you have a lot on your plate. You may be tempted to skim this section for action items. Powerfully committing is your foundational, supreme action. If you don't give yourself the few minutes you need to activate your commitment, how

If it feels awkward, lean in, I say! **Move past that cynical noise.**

can you expect to change? I've written your permission slip to chill for the few minutes you'll need to get this done. I stuffed it in your locker if you're looking for it.

Are you ready to slam your wizard staff into the ground, Gandalf? *Excellent.*

You'll need your favorite journal and pen. Bonus points for ritualizing this process. You can leverage the energy of a new moon, which strengthens intention setting, and/or use a candle, incense, or your favorite essential oils. This is big and benefits from metaphysical assistance. Every intention we bring will help overcome the very real resistance that's coming. The whole process comes down to your written and spoken word. This is the activation. We want God, Goddess, the Universe, maybe your neighbors, and our subconscious minds to hear us, and to respond. Better yet, *feel us and respond.* To achieve the deepest possible resonance, get highly intentional with this language.

Speak this aloud to yourself as you write it down. If it feels awkward, lean in, I say! Move past that cynical noise. Take a few deep breaths. And now...

Permission Slip to Chill

Because I deeply love myself, everyone around me, and All That Is, I, [name], am giving myself the Permission to Chill. Not only in this moment but in all moments moving forward, especially when I need it most.

I am committed to creating space within and around me at all times. I choose the radical, defiant act of slowing down. Of seeking and finding stillness. I will create any and all habits I need to honor my commitment to Chill.

> *When I fail, I will pick right up where I left off. I
> expect this journey to be challenging at times, so I have
> zero attachment to the process. When my path bends
> fully vertical, I am willing to climb.*
>
> *My work is to repeatedly give myself this permission,
> as many times as necessary—starting now. In doing so,
> I am allowing and receiving all assistance. I release any
> predictable resistance as it shows up.*
>
> *From this moment forward, Permission to Chill is
> granted.*
>
> *And so it is.*

Rinse and repeat this activation for the remaining permissions, adapting the language for each.

Bonus points: Read aloud the invocations at the end of each of the symbology chapters (pages 60, 96, 131, and 171).

Double bend-and-snap bonus points: Acquire, then generously apply our custom-blended essential oils for each of the 4 Permissions. Our resident healer and essential oils intuitive, Shauna Wetenkamp, designed each of the 4 Permissions oils for our Epic Retreats. They are gorgeously powerful. Like you. Visit ThisEpicLife.com for more information.

2. Declare and fulfill

In coaching, there's a simple yet powerful concept: declare and fulfill.

A declaration is simply a statement of *I will* [what?] *by* [when?].

Sometimes creating something new in our lives is literally as simple as declaring it. And exactly as hard as showing up to fulfill it. When we make a declaration, I believe the Universe hears it and mobilizes to support us. Resources and allies appear to help us fulfill our declaration.

Declaration is a summoning force. Call the lightning, Mighty Thor! What by when?

EXPAND
YOUR AWARENESS

What is one powerful declaration you can make right now?

Examples of declarations that have been fulfilled:

I will book our epic family vacation by May 1.

I will quit drinking by Memorial Day weekend.

I will lose 33 pounds by December 31.

I will create a breakthrough in Profound Friendship by April 15.

3. Start small

This is the conscious incompetence phase of your journey. Creating a new habit is a quest. I regularly witness powerful executives, who have no problem doubling their sales goals, struggle to honor even the smallest commitments to themselves. Whatever goal you've been avoiding, break it down to its most ridiculously small component. For example, a client who has a hard time getting enough sleep committed to buying a new pillow. (And he crushed it.)

So what if it feels like placing a Wiffle ball on the T-ball stand? Swing for the bleachers, champ!

4. Choose consistency over duration

When we start small, we set the foundation for consistency. Thousands of people, some of whom are busier than you, haven't missed a day of meditation in four or five years. All by living this mantra: consistency over duration. Your ego will squawk that you're not going deep enough, or bench-pressing enough weight. *That woman meditates for three hours a day and vacations in Tahiti! How will I ever catch up?* You won't. Consistency is the only metric.

This week, how many sessions (or workouts) would be an improvement on last week? If you had to, could you show up daily? Our addictive tendencies can be transformed into great allies. Are you willing to trade a less desirable habit for something that better serves you? I've seen plenty of daily addictions transformed into disciplined, healthy habits.

When you tap into the cumulative power of consistency, there are compounding returns on your investment of time. Show up daily and invest that nickel or dime (representing five or ten minutes). Move on with your day. You'll be shocked by what you accomplish in a month, in a decade.

5. Celebrate and savor

"What will you do to celebrate?" I heard this question constantly from my coach, and it bugged me. Bob would always ask it, even after some benign little win. We celebrate birthdays or big promotions. We celebrate substantial milestones but rarely the little ones. When anyone meditates for seven straight days, this is cause for celebration. It doesn't have to be some gala affair.

Celebration is a form of savoring that tells the Universe, "More please!" There are countless ways to celebrate that don't require spending any money or sending out invitations. Celebration is a form of self-love. At the very least, acknowledge what you accomplished and share it with someone. This simple act will create a bubble of momentum that drives more and more consistency.

If you don't celebrate periodically, I just might have to show up with (biodegradable) glitter cannons and a ticker tape parade.

6. When you fail, just get back up

Those who succeed in creating new habits learn it's a messy dance between the way things are and what could be. When you miss a day, just cut the crap and get back to it. When a newly sober person relapses, it's a big deal. Their sleeping dragon awakens and may never quiet back down. One drink can explode into victimization and shame. As appealing as the status quo tasted in having that drink, it's the head noise that hijacked their commitment. Getting back up may feel like work, but it's actually self-compassion. Quietly build what could be. Session by session. Near beer by near beer.

Resolutions can be tricky. Absolutes beg to be broken. We go in wanting to believe we can change and then falter the moment life gets in the way. It helps to assume we'll go sideways at some point. If you master a new habit out of the gate, that's excellent. For the rest of us mortals, we'll need to release the shame, pile on self-compassion, and quietly get back to work.

If it didn't happen today, the reason doesn't matter. Your commitment matters. Plan on honoring your commitment tomorrow. Failure isn't missing a day. Failure is not showing up again.

When you tap into the cumulative power of consistency, there are compounding returns on your investment of time.

7. Deepen, expand

To win the game of personal change requires a commitment to deepen and expand your practice indefinitely. An eternal student never loses that spark to go deeper. We've built the muscle memory to keep showing up. Now it's about giving more and more of ourselves. There's no participation award. Just bigger and bigger investments of our time and attention. You may have heard the saying, "A black belt is a white belt who never quit."

IN CLOSING, A GARDEN OF DEVOTION

BRING IT in.

Take a knee.

Nice hustle out there; you're playing with tons of heart.

Your glow is the differentiator. Between frenemies or conscious, radiant living. Between what is and what will be.

Each permission has its own path to mastery. Plenty of seekers and eventual masters walked that path to the end, and they'll tell you they've just begun. Doubling down in our efforts will prove there's no limit to the benefits we can experience, how much we can give, and how much we can receive.

At the end of our lives, it's the care and attention we gave. To others, to ourselves. To love these bodily temples enough to welcome in Spirit. The devotion of time and attention were the least we could do. Like a grandparent's flower garden.

Devotion is discipline but with fervor. Years of showing up compounded by feeling the feels. Reverence. The warm glow of steady growth. Deepening laugh lines on our sun-kissed faces. From activating our commitments to starting small through the full arc of indefinite expansion. Creating lasting, positive change is what our Creator intended.

Every small victory is something no one can ever take away.

In our willingness
to choose beyond
our default patterns,
we tune out our
frenemies and slide
The Source fader
over. **We begin
to glow**.

THROW THE SWITCH. NOW.

Which of the 4 Permissions represents the biggest potential breakthrough for you or your team?

This Epic Life offers group programs, one-on-one coaching, and transcendent retreat experiences to support and activate all 4 Permissions.

Please include the subject "Throw the Switch" and email us at glow@thisepiclife.com.

For written correspondence, or to share mix tapes, etc.:

This Epic Life
PO Box 22554
Akron, OH 44302

WE GOT THIS.

thisepiclife.com/glow

ADDITIONAL RESOURCES

Chill
Create your unbreakable meditation habit:
thisepiclife.com/30

Feel all the feels
The 4 Permissions manifesto and activation oils:
thisepiclife.com/manifesto

Glow in the dark
Design and deliver your ideal morning:
thisepiclife.com/morning

Glow in the light
The 7 Commitments—to scaling a powerhouse team or
company culture: thisepiclife.com/teams

NOTES

‒‒‒‒‒‒

THE 4 PERMISSIONS

1   Often incorrectly attributed to Viktor Frankl, the quote
    actually originates with Stephen Covey in 1969, after being
    inspired by Rollo May. See "Between Stimulus and Response
    There Is a Space. In That Space Is Our Power to Choose Our
    Response," Quote Investigator, February 18, 2018, https://
    quoteinvestigator.com/2018/02/18/response; Rollo May,
    "Freedom and Responsibility Re-examined," in *Behavioral
    Science and Guidance: Proposals and Perspectives*, edited by
    Esther Lloyd-Jones and Esther M. Westervelt (New York:
    Bureau of Publications, Teachers College, Columbia
    University, 1963), 101–2.

2   Lexico: Powered by Oxford, s.v. "dark star," accessed February
    25, 2021, https://www.lexico.com/definition/dark_star.

3   *Saturday Night Live*, season 25, episode 16, "Christopher
    Walken," directed by Beth McCarthy-Miller and James
    Signorelli, aired April 8, 2000, on NBC.

THE PEACE WE CRAVE

1   Jim Collins, *Good to Great: Why Some Companies Make the Leap
    and Others Don't* (New York: Harper Collins, 2001).

2   Earl Nightingale, *The Strangest Secret*, read by the author,
    Nightingale-McHugh Company, phonograph record, 1957;
    Earl Nightingale, *The Strangest Secret* (Shippensburg, PA: Sound
    Wisdom, 2019).

3   Brother Bhumananda in conversation with the author, August
    2015. Brother Bhumananda and I spoke on the phone as I
    prepped a talk, "What Steve Jobs Learned from Paramahansa
    Yogananda," which I delivered at Wisdom 2.0 Business in New
    York City in September 2015.

PAUSE BUTTON SYMBOLOGY

I   Steven Frears, dir., *High Fidelity* (Burbank, CA: Buena Vista
    Pictures, 2000), 113 min.
2   "Between Stimulus and Response There Is a Space. In
    That Space Is Our Power to Choose Our Response," Quote
    Investigator, February 18, 2018, https://quoteinvestigator.
    com/2018/02/18/response; Rollo May, "Freedom and
    Responsibility Re-examined," in *Behavioral Science and
    Guidance: Proposals and Perspectives*, edited by Esther Lloyd-
    Jones and Esther M. Westervelt (New York: Bureau of
    Publications, Teachers College, Columbia University, 1963),
    101–2.

IF CHILL IS THE BALM, VUCA IS THE RASH

I   Carl Bianco, "How Your Heart Works," HowStuffWorks.com
    (April 1, 2000), https://health.howstuffworks.com/human-
    body/systems/circulatory/heart.htm.
2   Ellie Fahy, "Blood Vessels: The 60,000 Mile Network
    Inside Us," 3D4 Medical Anatomy (platform by Elsevier),
    https://3d4medical.com/blog/blood-vessels-the-60000-mile-
    network-inside-us-anatomy-snippets.

DISCERNMENT IS WHAT WE'RE AFTER

I   Richard J. Davidson and Antoine Lutz, "Buddha's Brain:
    Neuroplasticity and Meditation," *IEEE Signal Processing
    Magazine* 25, no. 1 (2008): 176–74, https://www.ncbi.nlm.nih.
    gov/pmc/articles/PMC2944261/?report=classic.
2   Ravindra P. Nagendra, Nirmala Maruthai, and Bindu M.
    Kutty, "Meditation and Its Regulatory Role on Sleep" (2006)
    Frontiers in Neurology 3, no. 54 (April 18, 2012): doi:10.3389/
    fneur.2012.00054.

3   Lance M. Dodes, *The Sober Truth: Debunking the Bad Science behind 12-Step Programs and the Rehab Industry* (Boston: Beacon Press, 2014).

GAME FACE, AND OTHER WAYS WE HIDE

1   *The Future of Jobs Report 2020* (Geneva: World Economic Forum, 2020), http://www3.weforum.org/docs/WEF_Future_of_Jobs_2020.pdf.
2   *The Future of Jobs: Employment, Skills and Workforce Strategy for the Fourth Industrial Revolution* (Geneva: World Economic Forum, 2016), http://www3.weforum.org/docs/WEF_Future_of_Jobs.pdf.
3   "Emotional Intelligence," Genos International, accessed February 23, 2021, https://www.genosinternational.com/emotional-intelligence/.
4   Robert Zemeckis, dir., *Back to the Future Part II* (Universal City, CA: Universal Pictures, 1989), 108 min.
5   "How to Manage Trauma," The National Council for Behavioral Health, accessed February 23, 2021, https://www.thenationalcouncil.org/wp-content/uploads/2013/05/Trauma-infographic.pdf?daf=375ateTbd56.
6   Chris Buck and Jennifer Lee, dir., *Frozen* (Burbank, CA: Walt Disney Studios Motion Pictures, 2013), 102 min.

A PATH BACK TO OBJECTIVITY

1   Pete Doctor, dir., *Inside Out* (Burbank, CA: Walt Disney Studios Motion Pictures, 2015), 95 min.
2   Alan S. Cowen, and Dacher Keltner, "Self-Report Captures 27 Distinct Categories of Emotion Bridged by Continuous Gradients," *Proceedings of National Academy of Sciences (PNAS)* 114, no. 38 (September 19, 2017): E7900–E7909, https://doi.org/10.1073/pnas.1702247114.

FEELING TO CREATE

1   Marshall B. Rosenberg, *Nonviolent Communication: A Language of Life* (Encinitas, CA: PuddleDancer Press, 2003).

2   Susan Piver's Enneagram workshops are transformative. She
    doesn't recommend any of the online assessments. See www.
    susanpiver.com.

LIGHTNING BOLT SYMBOLOGY

1   Robert Zemeckis, *Back to the Future* (Universal City, CA:
    Universal Pictures, 1985), 116 min.

DARKNESS—FEAR OR FUEL?

1   Earl Nightingale, *The Strangest Secret*, read by the author,
    Nightingale-McHugh Company, phonograph record, 1957;
    Earl Nightingale, *The Strangest Secret* (Shippensburg, PA: Sound
    Wisdom, 2019).
2   Martin Luther King Jr., *Strength to Love* (Minneapolis: Fortress
    Press, 2010).
3   Frederick Perls, Ralph Hefferline, and Paul Goodman, *Gestalt
    Therapy: Excitement and Growth in the Human Personality*
    (Gouldsboro, ME: The Gestalt Journal Press, Inc., 1991).
4   Gay Hendricks, *The Big Leap: Conquer Your Hidden Fear and
    Take Life to the Next Level* (New York: HarperOne, 2010).
5   Hendricks, *The Big Leap*, 17.
6   Hendricks, *The Big Leap*, 17–18.

OUR GLOW ORIGINATES FROM SOMEPLACE ELSE

1   Accomplishment Coaching™, Essence conversation (All rights
    reserved), https://www.accomplishmentcoaching.com.
2   Malala Yousafzai, *I Am Malala: The Girl Who Stood Up
    for Education and Was Shot by the Taliban* (London: Orion
    Publishing Group Ltd., 2013), 46.

WHAT HAVE YOU BEEN PREPARING FOR?

1   Yogapedia, s.v. "Seva Yoga," last updated April 9, 2016, https://
    www.yogapedia.com/definition/6201/seva-yoga.
2   Daya Mata, *Only Love: Living the Spiritual Life in a Changing
    World* (Los Angeles: Self-Realization Fellowship, 1976), 9.

WE ARE ONE OF MANY

1   Marc Blaushild interview with Kristoffer Carter, "Marc
    Blaushild: A 3rd Generation CEO on Living Your Values,
    Mastering Time, and Creating Legacy (#5)," *This Epic Life*
    podcast, 46:04, https://www.thisepiclife.com/marc-blaushild.

FINDING THE LIGHT, AND HOW TO GLOW IN IT

1   Pema Chödrön, *When Things Fall Apart: Heart Advice for
    Difficult Times* (Boulder, CO: Shambhala Publications, 1997,
    2016).

2   Paramahansa Yogananda, *Metaphysical Meditations* (Los Angeles:
    Self-Realization Fellowship, 1967).

THE MEASURE OF A LEADER

1   Michael Bungay Stanier, *The Coaching Habit: Say Less, Ask
    More & Change the Way You Lead Forever* (Toronto: Box of
    Crayons Press/Vancouver, Page Two, 2016); Michael Bungay
    Stanier, *The Advice Trap: Be Humble, Stay Curious & Change
    the Way You Lead Forever* (Toronto: Box of Crayons Press/
    Vancouver, Page Two, 2020).

PERMISSION TO SUCK (FOR JUST A BIT)

1   Paul R. Curtiss and Phillip W. Warren, *The Dynamics of Life
    Skills Coaching* (Prince Albert, SK: Training Research and
    Development Station, Dept. of Manpower and Immigration,
    1973), 89, https://files.eric.ed.gov/fulltext/ED087852.pdf.

THE 7 (COMPASSIONATE) LAWS OF PERSONAL CHANGE

1   Ovid III, *Metamorphoses, Books 1–8*, trans. by Frank Justus
    Miller, rev. by G. P. Goold (Cambridge, MA: Harvard University
    Press, 1984).

ACKNOWLEDGMENTS

DRAFTING A book can be like harvesting a slab of granite from the earth and then dragging it through the cold cafeteria of conscious incompetence. And then comes the chiseling! By Grace, armies of angels arrive to assist. Far too many to name. Named and unnamed, please accept my deepest gratitude for your impact.

For tactical book design, editing, marketing, and publishing: this literally wouldn't have been possible without Page Two. To Trena White and her genius team of Kind Canadians: Thanks for believing, and delivering something special. Kendra Ward, the best editor in the business: you elevated everything. Praise Yoga! Rony Ganon, Madame President. Chris Brandt, and that beard, though. Taysia Louie and Peter Cocking for Glowing in the Fonts. Crissy Calhoun for copyedits. Steph VanderMeulen for Gen X gut checks. Lorraine Toor for distribution magic.

To Theresa O'Connor: you were the first to see this book, which made me believe. To all teachers, coaches, and mentors, physical and non-physical. Christine Sachs MCC, for coaching P2G into being. Accomplishment Coaching. Alice Bandy, you continue to guide this work. I'll love you and miss you forever.

To Jonathan, Stephanie, and the Good Life Project™ family. Karen Wright, Cynthia Morris, and Laura Neff: the three reasons I'm a coach. Robert "Pizza Bobby" Conlin. Book nerds: Charlie Gilkey (Costa Rica forever), Susan Piver, Todd Sattersten of Bard Press, Cynthia (again), Ani DiFranco (long live the queen!), and Eric Klein. For your generosity around my Big Honkin' Book Dreams. Matt Horak for his genius comic visuals.

No ideas are tested or refined, or funded, without our incredible clients—past, present, future. Your photos hung nearby while I wrote this book to you. Whether we worked together last week or last decade, I hope you notice your divine fingerprints all over this book.

Thanks to the Circuit Board of advisors and allies. Your input and enthusiasm have been a Godsend.

My seven parental units: Gary, Valerie, Wendy, Wayne, Dolli, Tom, and Harvey. Our Detention band family.

My team: Shauna Wetenkamp, our favorite Wonderbeast. Michele Morales. Layla Laser. Wizard Phil. Troy Young. Our staff of world-class coaches.

To the Carter kids: Frankie, Leon, Elliott. You remind me daily to find every reason to glow.

And first, there was Gayle. Nothing is possible without you. Head coach of Carter Force 5. I love you and remain in awe of your light.

ACKNOWLEDGMENTS

First, and last: thank you to the Omniscient Father, Divine Mother, Great Ones, and beloved Gurudeva— for your infinite love and encouragement.

"From joy we came,
for joy we live,
in that Sacred Joy
we'll someday melt away."

PARAMAHANSA YOGANANDA

ABOUT THE AUTHOR

KRISTOFFER SAT for his ninth-grade yearbook photo rocking a very tightly permed mullet. He blames his friend Big Dave for talking him into it.

LinkedIn didn't feel like the proper venue to share this important revelation. You'll find anything you need to know about KC's professional and spiritual adventures on ThisEpicLife.com.

Connect directly with Kristoffer on LinkedIn or Facebook. Connect deeply with his teachings on Insight Timer. His mom made his name harder to spell, yet somehow easier to find in social networks. Search "Kristoffer Carter."

KC chills, feels, and glows in Akron, Ohio, with "The Carter Force 5"—his wife of twenty-two years, Gayle, and their three remarkable spawn, Elliott (17), Frankie (13), and Leon (10).

CPSIA information can be obtained
at www.ICGtesting.com
Printed in the USA
BVHW070931051021
618190BV00005BA/71

9 781774 581582